A-Z
Sparkling Illustrations

A-Z
Sparkling Illustrations

*Stories, Anecdotes,
and Humor for Speakers*

Stephen Gaukroger

Nick Mercer

BakerBooks

A Division of Baker Book House Co
Grand Rapids, Michigan 49516

Previously published by Scripture Union in the United Kingdom as *Frogs in Cream* (1990) and *Frogs II* (1993).

Published by Baker Books
a division of Baker Book House Company
P.O. Box 6287, Grand Rapids, MI 49516-6287

Printed in the United States of America

Library of Congress Cataloging-in-Publication Data

Gaukroger, Stephen.
    A–Z sparkling illustrations : stories, anecdotes, and humor for speakers / Stephen Gaukroger, Nick Mercer.
      p. cm.
    Originally published: Frogs in cream and Frogs II. London : Scripture Union, 1990 and 1993 respectively.
    ISBN 0-8010-9038-5 (pbk.)
    1. Public speaking. 2. Wit and humor. I. Mercer, Nick. II. Title.
PN4193.I5G38 1997
082—dc21   97-21592

For current information about all releases from Baker Book House, visit our web site:
                    http://www.bakerbooks.com

Dedicated to Spurgeon's College,
where learning and laughter meet.

Contents

Acknowledgments

We are grateful to all those from whom we have borrowed material for this collection—both inadvertently and "vertently"!

We gratefully acknowledge the many speakers—good, bad and indifferent—whom it has been our pleasure to listen to over the years. Especially those who know how to tell a story.

Introduction

This book is written in the hope that sermons, speeches and talks of every kind can be given a new lease on life. It arises from the belief that a good illustration reaches parts of a congregation that other homiletic techniques cannot reach.

This collection of illustrative material is offered to the planet in the hope of worldwide renewal, restoration and revival. Failing that, we'd settle for a lot fewer congregations and audiences being bored to death by worthy, yet dull, presentations. For too many listeners, the *Te Deum* has been replaced by *tedium*. The Good News deserves better!

Stephen Gaukroger

Nick Mercer

Part 1

The Art of Illustration and Storytelling

Finding and Using Illustrations

To most modern congregations, illustrations are like the ketchup on the burger, the cream on the strawberries or the chocolate flakes in the ice cream. You can exist without them, but it's so much tastier when they are there! Most speakers know the value of good illustrations—but where do you get them? Well, you could:

- Develop your powers of observation. Daily life is a rich source of funny, sad and poignant incidents. Train yourself to look for them.
- Keep pen and paper handy. Write down possible illustrations as you come across them on TV, in the paper, in the shower or in general reading.
- Read biographies. People are interested in other people—particularly famous other people!
- "Steal" them from other speakers!
- Use the little stories at the bottom of the page in the *Readers' Digest.*

Illustrations usually need to illustrate, but occasionally they can be used effectively simply to give the congregation breathing space between the meatier sections of a sermon or talk. A short, illustrative "mental break" is likely to increase the length of time the congregation or audience can concentrate.

Don't use too many illustrations, tell inappropriate jokes or pretend something happened to *you* when you got the story from a book! Timing is essential to watch, too: beware of giving the right illustration at the wrong time in the message. As a general rule, the nearer you get to the end of the talk, the less likely is humor to be appropriate.

Take up these suggestions, avoid the pitfalls, and then your illustrations won't be like ketchup on strawberries or chocolate flakes in your burgers!

Humor and the Bible

The Bible is a profoundly serious collection of writings, yet it is also full of humor of every type, although this is sometimes lost in translation or through familiarity. A person with a good sense of humor almost always has good self-insight. Perhaps this is why so many of the Bible's writers used humor to comment incisively and memorably on issues of immense personal and national concern.

The Bible's humor ranges through:

- the *irony* of the Tower of Babel, built to reach "up" to heaven—and God arranges an outing to go "down" to see it (Genesis 11:4–5);
- the *pun* on Ehud, the left-handed Benjamite (Benjamin—"son of my right hand"; Judges 3:15);
- the "lavatorial" *sarcasm* of Elijah on Carmel, mocking the no-show of the god Baal—"perhaps he's in the bathroom?" (1 Kings 18:27);
- the *exaggeration* of Jesus—"It's easier to get a camel through the eye of a needle than to get a rich person into heaven!" (Luke 18:25);

- and even the *risqué innuendo* of Paul's barbed comment about some Jewish Christians who insisted that believers must be circumcised—"If only the knife would slip . . . !" (Galatians 5:12).

If preaching is in part truth through personality, then we, like the writers of the Bible, must use every aspect of our personalities, including the gift of humor, to communicate God's truth.

Good and Bad Uses of Humor

The Bible's humor is generally heavy on irony and light on sarcasm. Preachers down through the ages have sometimes taken the easy way out, though, and majored on sarcasm while ducking the harder work of irony. Even Luther and Calvin stooped to this. Spurgeon, the nineteenth-century prince of preachers who pulled in vast crowds, also peppered his sermons with every form of wit—irony, pun, hyperbole, litotes, anecdote, parody, caricature, satire . . . and even a little sarcasm.

How can we use humor for the best advantage of our message, rather than take advantage of others or of our position with a captive audience? Here are some suggestions of things to avoid and of ways to use humor.

Humor at Its Worst . . .

- is attention-seeking and reflects self-centeredness.
- sidetracks a good raconteur by encouraging him to make the audience laugh even more!

- distracts an audience if used unthinkingly. A witticism may pop into the speaker's head, but speaking it out may destroy the atmosphere the Spirit was building.
- can be disastrous if accidental. For instance, a spoonerism ("Who is a gardening pod like Thee . . .") or a *double entendre* as a result of not being streetwise in the current use of language ("It was a gay evening . . .") can cause the audience to roll around in hysterics while your serious message is lost for ever.
- is pastorally insensitive. Acts which leave people devastated, such as abortion, rape and child abuse, should never be referred to humorously. A wide range of other subjects, including death, sex, homosexuality, feminism, politics and foreigners, can only be used with the utmost care and where you really know your audience.
- goes down like a pork pie in a synagogue if humor doesn't come naturally to you. If you're not comfortable using humor, neither will your congregation or audience be!

Humor at Its Best . . .

- illustrates the point.
- gains rapport with the audience, especially if they are unknown to you and to each other.
- releases unhelpful tension among the listeners, perhaps by defusing the pressure of a difficult subject, breaking up a long sermon or simply giving you and the audience time for a few deep breaths and a readjustment of clothes!
- breaks through the listeners' defenses, making them more open to what God has to say to them.
- brings people down to earth, reminding us of humankind's foolishness and peeling away the pompos-

ity and humbug with which we surround ourselves. Humor helps us see our true, petty and paradoxical selves: full of noble aspirations and sordid fantasies— just like an impressive cathedral whose spire points us to heaven but whose gargoyles laugh down at us.

- identifies us with our culture. Humor is one of the most powerful vehicles of communication in late twentieth-century Western culture. People expect it, and it gets through to them. Watch TV; listen to the radio; read the papers, popular magazines and books; and see how the advertisers use humor to sell their wares.

- is one of God's greatest medicines for tired and anxious minds. As Malcolm Muggeridge, the former editor of *Punch* and a late-in-life convert, commented, "Next to mystical enlightenment, [laughter] is the most precious gift and blessing that comes to us on earth."

The Art of Storytelling

"Tell us a story!" Children have cried this to adults in every culture since language began. And for the grownups, the soap operas continue to pull the largest audiences. Much of the Bible came to us by way of storytelling. Parents told children the great stories of God's dealings with his people; they learned them by heart and told them to their children. Other stories were written with great care and stylistic purpose, like Jonah and Job, Ruth and Esther, but written primarily for reading out loud and remembering. The Bible was never penned as a modern study text; it was set down to be proclaimed by the leaders and acted on by all as it penetrated the heart and mind.

This is why Jesus told stories: those memorable parables and word pictures, stories about the Good Shepherd, and the Vine and so much that many Christians can still recite from memory.

There is a power in storytelling that goes beyond the words themselves. When you play with computers, you are sometimes aware that there is a language behind the language that you type onto the screen—it is called a "deep-level" language, and there are even deeper levels behind that language. In the same way, stories communicate at a level that is much deeper than the mere logic and syntax of the sentences. There is a deep mystery behind words, just as Jesus, the Word, is embedded at the heart of the mystery of the Trinity. Many preachers fail to appreciate this and deliver the word of God in a framework worthy of a government regulation. In a way, all preaching is—or should be—storytelling.

Stories can transport us to another realm, whether it is Revelation's Christ in glory, or Adam's brush with the angel of the flaming sword, or Jospeh's many-colored coat; and there, amazingly, they can reshape our lives.

Stories can often bring out old truths in new ways. This has been the success of *Peanuts,* or *The Little Prince,* or *Jonathan Livingstone Seagull,* or that children's classic, *The Velveteen Rabbit.* Margery Williams is only restating a biblical truth, but because she says it in a different way, it comes across with fresh power:

> The Skin Horse had lived longer in the nursery than any others. He was so old that his brown coat was bald in patches and showed the seams underneath, and most of the hairs in his tail had been pulled out to string bead necklaces. . . .
>
> "What is REAL?" asked the Rabbit one day. . . "Does it mean having things that buzz inside you and a stick-out handle?"
>
> "Real isn't how you are made," said the Skin Horse. "It's a thing that happens to you. When a child loves you for a long, long time, not just to play with, but REALLY loves you, then you become Real."
>
> "Does it hurt?" asked the Rabbit.
>
> "Sometimes," said the Skin Horse, for he was always truthful. "When you are Real you don't mind being hurt."
>
> "Does it happen all at once, like being wound up," he asked, "or bit by bit?"
>
> "It doesn't happen all at once," said the Skin Horse. "You become. It takes a long time. That's why it doesn't often happen to people who break easily, or who have sharp edges, or who have to be carefully kept. Generally, by the time you are Real, most of your hair has been loved off, and your eyes drop

out and you get loose in the joints and very shabby. But these things don't matter at all, because once you are Real you can't be ugly, except to people who don't understand."
(From *The Velveteen Rabbit*, Margery Williams, New York: Holt, Rinehart and Winston, 1983, 4–5.)

Hints for Storytellers

- Be utterly convinced of what you are saying. Act as if the fiction were a reality. If you've ever been to Disney World, you will know that all those people dressed as Mickey Mouse or Donald Duck or Snow White will never break the pretense, whatever you say to them. That is what makes the place so enchanting. Never apologize for the story or feel "silly" while you are reading it.
- Never be bored by the material, however familiar it is to you.
- In a culture that is not very well tuned to poetry and myth, I usually give some words of explanation beforehand in order to help people know what they are looking for. I was amazed, when speaking with a student who had read C. S. Lewis's *The Lion, The Witch and The Wardrobe*, to realize that he had not grasped any of the Christian imagery in the story.
- Learn by heart the opening and the ending and, if possible, the middle!
- Use regional accents or other voices if you can do it convincingly and if it helps the storytelling.
- Body language is still very important, even if you are reading from a script. Use your hands and eyes to draw people into the story.
- Use appropriate background music occasionally: classical guitar or other instruments, but not playing Christian songs—this is a distraction which encourages people to "sing along" in their minds. I once read the

Seven Trumpets of the Apocalypse from the book of Revelation to impromptu accompaniment by a professional pianist. It brought home the mystery and awe of those obscure verses in a startling way.

- Find gifted people who can tell stories better than you. The change in voice can increase the impact. I can still remember a school teacher who learned and recited T. S. Eliot's *Journey of the Magi*. When he got to the end of the last stanza, there was a stunned silence.

Hints for Storywriters

- Impromptu stories are usually poor and muddled unless you are a really accomplished raconteur. The best off-the-cuff comments are always carefully premeditated!
- Listen to good storytellers. There are plenty on the radio, and many tapes are available that you can listen to in the car. Garrison Keillor (Lake Wobegon) is a master writer and storyteller, bringing simple truths home from people's everyday lives.
- Remember that most short stories or poems, like Jesus' parables, make only one main point. The gruesome children's stories of the Brothers Grimm follow this rule, and so does any episode of *The Waltons*. Don't get sidetracked by obfuscatory secondary points!
- When possible, develop your own style and use recurring themes and catchphrases: "Once upon a time . . ." "And they all lived happily ever after . . ." "It has been a quiet week in Lake Wobegon . . ." "Truly, truly I say to you, the kingdom of heaven is like . . ." I started all my children's talks in one church with the sing-song litany: "Good morning, children." "Good morning, Mr. Mer-cer."

- Try writing your own parables to bring out afresh some
  of the startling twists in familiar Bible parables or pas-
  sages. The original hearers of the story of the Pharisee
  and the tax-collector thought the Pharisee was the
  goody. But we all know he's the baddy as soon as the
  story starts. And the title "The Good Samaritan" gives
  the game away right from the start. For Jesus' audience,
  a good Samaritan was a contradiction in terms!

The Creator has made us creative beings—in his own image.
Storytelling is a way to create and recreate, and through the
Spirit's mysterious working to help shape people's lives to the
truth of the Gospel, the Greatest Story ever told.

Stories are the real life changers, for they *do* produce. Their
first and most significant product is conversion. They also
confront and change lives. They motivate to holiness, to
prayer, and to a loving and continuing affair with Scripture
(Calvin Miller, *Spirit, Word, and Story*, Baker, 1996, p. 155).

Part 2

An Alphabetical Collection of Stories, Illustrations, and Anecdotes

Abilities—Hitherto Undiscovered

A motorist who drove his Reliant Robin three-wheeler on the M20 at 105 miles per hour was fined £150 for speeding and banned from driving for twenty-one days. Magistrates at West Malling, Kent, heard that police following the driver were so amazed that they had the speedometer of their patrol car tested. The driver, a laborer, who was also ordered to pay £80 costs, said after the hearing that he bought the V-registration Reliant for £500, and "would not change it for anything."

Age

Growing old isn't so bad when you consider the alternative.

Maurice Chevalier

Aging

The seven ages of man: spills, drills, thrills, bills, ills, pills, wills.

Richard J. Needham

Lord, thou knowest better than I know myself that I am growing older. Keep me from getting too talkative and thinking I must say something on every subject and on every occasion.

Release me from craving to straighten out everybody's affairs. Teach me the glorious lesson that, occasionally, it is possible that I may be mistaken.

Make me thoughtful, but not moody; helpful, but not bossy; for thou knowest, Lord, that I want a few friends at the end.

Someone is old if he or she is twenty years older than yourself.

◎   ◎   ◎

Little girl to old man with grey beard: "Were you in the ark?"
"Goodness, no!"
Pause.
"Then why weren't you drowned?"

◎   ◎   ◎

Three signs of getting old:
1. Greying hair.
2. Memory loss.
And 3. . . . er . . . er . . .

◎   ◎   ◎

Beatitudes for the Aged

Blessed are they who understand
My faltering step and palsied hand.
Blessed are they who know my ears today
Must strain to catch the things they say.
Blessed are they who seem to know
My eyes are dim and wits are slow.
Blessed are they who look away
When coffee was spilt on the table today.
Blessed are they with a cheery smile,
Who stop to chat for a little while.
Blessed are they who never say,
"You've told that story twice today."
Blessed are they who know the way
To bring back memories of yesterday.
Blessed are they who make it known
I'm loved, respected, and not alone.
Blessed are they who ease the days
On my journey home in loving ways.

Agnosticism

Did you hear about the agnostic, dyslexic insomniac who lay awake at night wondering, "Is there a Dog?"

Alive Again!

A pastor's son was driving through the bush to Uige when UNITA soldiers forced him to take them with him. He protested that the brakes on the vehicle were no good. They disbelieved him until they came to a steep hill. The soldiers jumped out, as did the driver, who then hid in the long grass. The jeep crashed at the bottom of the hill and the soldiers set fire to it.

People saw it and word got to the pastor in Luanda that his son had been killed. So in the church they held a funeral thanksgiving service for him—but the son turned up in the middle of it. "This my son was dead and is alive again!"

Appearances (Which Can Be Deceptive)

A bishop and a student were travelling together on a small plane. Suddenly, the captain announced that the plane was ditching and told the passengers to bail out—apologizing that there were only two parachutes between the three of them. Immediately, the Brain of Britain grabbed one and jumped out. The student seemed remarkably unperturbed, but nevertheless, the bishop told him that since he was old and prepared to meet his God, the student should take the other parachute. And then he asked him, "How come you're so calm, anyway?" And the student replied, "Well, the Brain of Britain just jumped out with my rucksack!"

Atheism

To you I'm an atheist. To God I'm the loyal opposition.

Woody Allen

Attitude

A group of German psychologists, physicians and insurance companies who cooperated on a research project designed to find the secret to long life and success, made a surprising discovery. The secret? Kiss your spouse each morning when you leave for work!

The meticulous German researchers discovered that men who kiss their wives every morning have fewer car accidents on their way to work than men who omit the morning kiss. The good-morning kissers miss less work because of sickness and earn twenty to thirty percent more money than non-kissers. How do they explain their findings? According to West Germany's Dr. Arthur Szabo, "A husband who kisses his wife every morning begins the day with a positive attitude."

Authority

The Captain on the bridge of a large naval ship saw a light ahead, set for collision with his vessel. He signalled to it: "Alter your course ten degrees south." The reply came back: "Alter *your* course ten degrees north."

The Captain then signalled: "Alter your course ten degrees south. I am a Captain." The reply came back: "Alter your course ten degrees north. I am a Seaman third-class."

The Captain, furious by now, signalled back: "Alter your course ten degrees south. I am a battleship!" The reply: "Alter your course ten degrees north. I am a lighthouse."

33

Baptism

There was the Baptist minister who, at his first baptism, became stagestruck. Standing in the pool with the candidate, he suffered a complete lapse of memory. He became so muddled that he forgot which sacrament he was administering. Eyes heavenward, he commanded: "Drink ye all of it!"

Church bulletin: On Tuesday afternoon there will be meetings in the north and south ends of the church. Children will be baptized at both ends.

Baptists

Billy Graham is sitting quietly in a restaurant one day when a holdup man comes in brandishing a gun. "Okay. I want everyone to file past me and hand me their wallets." When Billy Graham arrives in front of the robber, the man recognizes him and motions the evangelist to put his wallet back in his pocket. "Put it away, Billy," he says. "We Baptists must stick together!"

At a Baptist church meeting there was heated discussion about changing the church's name from Puddlington Baptist Church to Puddlington Christian Church.

Eventually, one old boy stood up and declared, "I've been a Baptist for over fifty years and nobody's going to start calling *me* a Christian!"

How many Baptists does it take to change a light bulb?
A church meeting and about two-and-a-half years.

Bible

The Bible is so good, if it isn't true it ought to be!

◎　　◎　　◎

A theologically liberal minister was visiting one of the elderly members of his congregation. He noticed that her Bible had hundreds of pages torn out of it, while many others had been cut up.

"What happened to your Bible?" he asked.

"Oh," she replied, "I just tear out all the bits you say we can't believe any more."

◎　　◎　　◎

No one ever graduates from Bible study until he meets its Author face to face.

Everett Harris

◎　　◎　　◎

Every Christian must refer always and everywhere to the Scriptures for all his choices, becoming like a child before it, seeking in it the most effective remedy against all his various weaknesses, and not daring to take a step without being illuminated by the divine rays of those words.

Pope John Paul II

The Ten Commandments

People nowadays treat the Ten Commandments like a history exam . . . they attempt only three.

Psalms and Proverbs

David and Solomon lived right merry lives.
One had a thousand concubines, the other a
thousand wives.
But when, as they were growing old, they
began to have their qualms,

The one wrote the Proverbs and the
other wrote the Psalms.

Beatitudes for the Twentieth Century (Matthew 5)

Blessed are the pushers, for they get on in the world.
Blessed are the hard-boiled, for they never let life hurt them.
Blessed are they who complain, for they get their way in
the end.
Blessed are the blasé, for they never worry over their own sins.
Blessed are the slave-drivers, for they get results.
Blessed are the trouble-makers, for they make people no-
tice them.

J. B. Phillips

◎   ◎   ◎

Melody in F (Luke 15: the story of the lost son)

Feeling footloose and frisky, a featherbrained fellow
Forced his fond father to fork over the farthings.
He flew far to foreign fields,
And frittered his fortune feasting fabulously with faithless
friends.

Fleeced by his fellows in folly, and facing famine,
He found himself a feed-flinger in a filthy farmyard.
Fairly famishing, he fain would have filled his frame
With foraged food from fodder fragments.

"Fooey! My father's flunkies fare far finer!"
The frazzled fugitive forlornly fumbled, frankly facing facts.
Frustrated by failure, and filled with foreboding,
He fled forthwith to his family.

Falling at his father's feet, he forlornly fumbled,
"Father, I've flunked, and fruitlessly forfeited family fellow-
ship favor."
The farsighted father, forestalling further flinching,

Frantically flagged the flunkies, "Fetch a fatling from the
   flock and fix a feast!"

The fugitive's fault-finding brother frowned
On this fickle forgiveness of former falderal.
But the faithful father figured,
"Filial fidelity is fine, but the fugitive is found!
Let flags be unfurled! Let fanfares flare!"

His father's forgiveness formed the foundation
For the former fugitive's future fortitude.

John's Gospel

John's Gospel is "like a magic pool where a child can pad-
dle and an elephant can swim."

Francis Moloney

Acts

If you can't convince 'em with Matthew, Mark, Luke or
John . . . hit 'em with the Acts!

Complete Bibles in 322 languages

The number of languages into which at least one book
of the Bible has been translated rose from 1,946 in 1990 to
1,978 in 1991, according to the United Bible Societies. In
1991, thirty-two languages received at least one book of the
Bible for the first time, the largest first-time number since
1987. Complete Bibles were made available in four languages for the first time: two in Zaire, one in Guatemala,
and one in Yugoslavia. That, as of the end of 1991, increases
the number of languages with complete Bibles to 322.

American Bible Society figures quoted in
Christianity Today, 6 April 1992

Bible—Ignorance Of

A religious education teacher asked a pupil, "Who knocked down the walls of Jericho?"

"I didn't, Sir; I was away last week."

So the teacher went to the headmaster. "Who knocked down the walls of Jericho?" he asked.

"I'm not sure," said the headmaster. "I'll come back to you on that one."

The headmaster wrote to the Minister of Education, "Who knocked down the walls of Jericho?" he asked.

Eventually he received the reply, "You just get the wall rebuilt, and we'll see that someone pays the bill."

Bible Study

The story is told of a South Sea Islander who proudly displayed his Bible to a GI during World War II. Rather disdainfully, the soldier commented, "We've grown out of that sort of thing." The Islander smiled and said, "It's a good thing we haven't. If it weren't for this book, you'd have been a meal by now!"

Books

If he shall not lose his reward who gives a cup of cold water to his thirsty neighbor, what will not be the reward of those who by putting good books into the hands of those neighbors give to them the fountains of eternal life?

Thomas à Kempis

A man goes into the cinema and buys a ticket for himself and his dog. The usher is amazed to see the dog laughing throughout the film. After the show she comments to the man as he leaves, "I was staggered to see your dog laughing at the film!" The man replies, "So was I. He hated the book!"

Brevity

A large dinner party was organized to pay homage to a distinguished man. He spoke to the host beforehand and asked whether, in response to the eulogy, he wanted him to give his short speech or his long speech. The host, not surprisingly, asked for the short speech.

At the close of the dinner and after all the words of praise, the guest stood up and said, "Thank you!"

The host approached him afterward and asked him what his long speech would have been. "Thank you very much!" he replied.

Brevity of Life

A notice from the obituary column:

DIED: Salvador Sanchez, 23, World Boxing Council featherweight champion and one of the sport's best fighters; of injuries after his Porsche 928 collided with two trucks, just north of Queretaro, Mexico. A school dropout at 16, Sanchez once explained, "I found out that I liked hitting people, and I didn't like school, so I started boxing." A peppery tactician, he wore opponents down for late-round knockouts. His record: 43–1–1. "I'd like to step down undefeated," he said last month. "I'm only 23 and I have all the time in the world."

Busyness

Busyness rapes relationships. It substitutes shallow frenzy for deep friendships. It promises satisfying dreams but delivers hollow nightmares. It feeds the ego but starves the

inner man. It fills a calendar or diary but fractures a family.
It cultivates a program but plows under priorities.

Charles Swindoll, *Killing Giants, Pulling Thorns*

Calling

As long as God gives me breath, I expect to preach the gospel!

Billy Graham

◎   ◎   ◎

The issue for me is not whether women should be in ministry. . . . The issue is whether those in ministry, women or men, have been called by God to be there!

Anne Graham Lotz

◎   ◎   ◎

There is no work better than another to please God; to pour water, to wash dishes, to be a cobbler, or an apostle: all is one.

William Tyndale

◎   ◎   ◎

God buries his workmen but carries on his work.

Charles Wesley

◎   ◎   ◎

While women weep, as they do now, I'll fight; while little children go hungry, I'll fight; while men go to prison, in and out, as they do now, I'll fight; while there is a drunkard left, while there is a poor, lost girl upon the streets, where there remains one dark soul without the light of God—I'll fight! I'll fight to the very end!

William Booth

◎   ◎   ◎

TO: Jesus, son of Joseph, woodcrafter
    Carpenter's Shop, Nazareth
FROM: Jordan Management Consultants, Jerusalem

Dear Sir:

Thank you for submitting the résumés of the twelve men you have picked for management positions in your new organization. All of them have now taken our battery of tests; we have not only run the results through our computer, but also arranged personal interviews for each of them with our psychologist and vocational aptitude consultant.

It is the staff opinion that most of your nominees are lacking in background, education and vocational aptitude for the type of enterprise you are undertaking. They do not have the team concept. We would recommend that you continue your search for persons of experience in managerial ability and proven capability.

Simon Peter is emotionally unstable and given to fits of temper.

Andrew has absolutely no qualities of leadership.

The two brothers, *James and John,* the sons of Zebedee, place personal interest above company loyalty.

Thomas demonstrates a questioning attitude that would tend to undermine morale.

We feel it is our duty to tell you that *Matthew* has been blacklisted by the Greater Jerusalem Better Business Bureau.

James, son of Alphaeus, and *Thaddaeus* definitely have radical leanings, and they both registered a high score on the manic-depressive scale.

One of the candidates, however, shows great potential. He is a man of ability and resourcefulness, meets people well, has a keen business mind and has contacts in high places. He is highly motivated, ambitious and responsible. We recommend *Judas Iscariot* as your controller and right-hand man. All of the other profiles are self-explanatory.

We wish you success in your new venture.

Calvary

Calvary is a telescope through which we look into the long vista of eternity and see the love of God breaking forth into time.

Martin Luther King, Jr.

Change

The seven last words of the church: "We've never done it that way before!"

◎   ◎   ◎

If the good Lord had wanted us to go metric, he would have had only ten apostles.

◎   ◎   ◎

Halfway through the church meeting of his tiny Irish congregation, the new minister had a quiet word with the church secretary. "Do you have a word in Celtic for *mañana*?" he asked. "Yes," replied the secretary, "but it lacks the sense of urgency."

◎   ◎   ◎

There are three types of people: those who make things happen, those who watch things happen, and those who haven't a clue what's happening!

◎   ◎   ◎

A Ghanaian newspaper is reputed to have recorded the following piece of news: "Ghana is to change over to driving on the right. The change will be made gradually."

◎   ◎   ◎

One minister to another at a fraternal: "I can't stand change, especially in the collection!"

◎   ◎   ◎

I have examined myself thoroughly and have come to the conclusion that I do not need to change much.

Sigmund Freud

Character

A scorpion, being a poor swimmer, asked a turtle to carry him on his back across a river.

"Are you mad?" exclaimed the turtle. "You'll sting me while I'm swimming and I'll drown!"

"My dear turtle," laughed the scorpion, "if I were to sting you, you would drown and I would go down with you! Now, where is the logic in that?"

"You're right!" cried the turtle. "Hop on!"

The scorpion climbed aboard, and halfway across the river he gave the turtle a mighty sting. As they both sank to the bottom, the turtle resignedly said, "Do you mind if I ask you something? You said there'd be no logic in your stinging me. Why did you do it?"

"It had nothing to do with logic," the drowning scorpion replied, sadly. "It's just my character."

◎　◎　◎

Character is what you are in the dark.

D. L. Moody

◎　◎　◎

The way to gain a good reputation is to endeavor to be what you desire to appear.

Socrates

◎　◎　◎

It is right to be contented with what we have, never with what we are.

Sir James Mackintosh

Charismatics

How many charismatics does it take to change a light bulb?

Five: one to change the bulb and four to share the experience.

Children

The learned teach the child; the wise listen to him.

◎   ◎   ◎

A man got talking to a new colleague and discovered he had six children.

"I wish *I* had six kids," he said ruefully.
"How many do you have, then?" asked his colleague.
"Twelve!"

"Christaholics"

Many Christians are only "Christaholics" and not disciples at all. Disciples are cross-bearers; they seek Christ. Christaholics seek happiness . . . There is no automatic joy. Christ is not a happiness capsule; he is the way to the Father.

Calvin Miller

Church

The frenzied activities of evangelical Christians have become legendary. Thankfully, someone has now revised the old nursery rhyme so that it fits today's picture:

> Mary had a little lamb,
> 'Twas given her to keep,
> But then it joined the Baptist Church
> And died for lack of sleep.

◎   ◎   ◎

In the thrombosis of the church, the minister is often the clot.

◎   ◎   ◎

Those who fail to plan, plan to fail.

◎ ◎ ◎

Those who aim at nothing are sure to hit it.

◎ ◎ ◎

A new vicar regularly spent five days of the week in the grave-yard, cutting the grass and tidying up. The church council eventually questioned him about this and he replied, "As five-sevenths of my income comes from the dead, I thought I'd spend five-sevenths of my time with them!"

◎ ◎ ◎

A slightly cynical minister, on his first flight in a jumbo jet, said that it reminded him of his church: several hundred people sitting back looking bored and a few stewards and crew members rushed off their feet!

◎ ◎ ◎

> Some go to church to take a walk;
> Some go to church to laugh and talk;
> Some go there to meet a friend;
> Some go there their time to spend;
> Some go there to meet a lover;
> Some go there a fault to cover;
> Some go there for speculation;
> Some go there for observation;
> Some go there to doze and nod;
> The wise go there to worship God.

◎ ◎ ◎

Have you heard about the man who said he didn't intend to come to church again? He had only been twice. The first time as a baby they had poured cold water over him and the second time they joined him for life to a nagging wife. "Well, watch out," said the vicar, "the next time you come, we may throw dirt in your face!"

Church Growth

Could it be that just a few church members are like Pat the Irishman . . . ?

Two Irishmen on a tandem eventually arrived, perspiring, at the top of the hill.

"That was a stiff climb, Pat," said one.

"It was that," said Pat, "and if I hadn't kept the brake on we would have gone backwards for sure."

Church Music

When a man from the country returned from a visit to the city, he told his wife, Mary, that he had gone to church and that the choir had sung an anthem.

Mary asked, "What's an anthem?"

Her husband replied, "Well, it's like this. If I said, 'Mary, the cows are in the corn,' that would be like a hymn. But if I said, "Oh Mary! Mary! Mary! The cows are in the corn, the Jersey cow, the Ayrshire cow, the Muley cow; all the cows, all the cows, the cows, the cows are in the corn, the corn, the corn,' then that would be an anthem!"

Anglican Digest

Circumstances

Adverse circumstances are like a feather bed: all right if you're on top!

Commitment

When the famous film director, Franco Zeffirelli, announced that he was planning to film the life of Christ from birth to resurrection, film stars offered their services and some travelled thousands of miles to location sites in Tunisia and Morocco.

James Mason journeyed from Switzerland to play Joseph of Arimathea. Rod Steiger left California to play Pontius Pilate, and Laurence Olivier flew from London to take the role of Nicodemus. Many big stars played in minor roles. Claudia Cardinale was the most determined of the stars. She persisted in asking the director for a part in the film, and when she was told that all that remained was the part of the adulteress whom Christ forgave, she accepted. She flew from her home in Rome to Tunisia, arrived on the set on a very hot day, put on her makeup and her costume, and spent five hours in the blistering heat before the cameras. The sum total of her speaking part was only three lines.

She was willing to pay a high price in terms of personal discomfort and sacrifice in order to say a few words in a film about Jesus.

Doug Barnett

⊚ ⊚ ⊚

I don't mind if my life goes in the service of the nation. If I die today, every drop of my blood will invigorate the nation.

Indira Gandhi, the night before she was assassinated by Sikh militants, 30 October 1984

⊚ ⊚ ⊚

We know what happens to people who stay in the middle of the road: they get run over.

Aneurin Bevan

⊚ ⊚ ⊚

Seen on a bumper sticker: "If you love Jesus, tithe! Any fool can honk!"

⊚ ⊚ ⊚

A group of clergymen were discussing whether or not they ought to invite Dwight L. Moody to their city. The success of the famed evangelist was brought to the attention of the men.

One unimpressed minister commented, "Does Mr. Moody have a monopoly on the Holy Ghost?"

Another man quietly replied, "No, but the Holy Ghost seems to have a monopoly on Mr. Moody."

Communication

The Rev. W. A. Spooner, the English scholar who died in 1930, was reputed to have had a dreadful habit of confusing his message in the process of giving it:

On one occasion he announced to his congregation that the next hymn would be, "From Iceland's greasy mountains."

At a wedding he told the groom, "It is kistomary to cuss the bride."

Calling on the dean of Christ Church he asked the secretary, "Is the bean dizzy?"

Giving the eulogy at a clergyman's funeral, he praised his departed colleague as a "shoving leopard to his flock."

In a sermon he warned his congregation, "There is no peace in a home where a dinner swells," meaning, of course, "where a sinner dwells."

Speaking to a group of farmers, Spooner intended to greet them as "sons of toil," but what came out was, "I see before me tons of soil."

A sign in three languages in the Swiss village of Chateau d'Oex shows the impossibility of arriving at common European standards. In English, it says, "Please do not pick the flowers." In German: "It is forbidden to pick the flowers." In

French: "Those who love the mountains, leave them their flowers."

The Times, 4 June 1992

⊚   ⊚   ⊚

In seventeenth-century England, the church was an important part of family life. In the small villages, the minister was personally acquainted with every member of his congregation and with their problems.

So it was natural that, one Sunday in Shropshire, Mrs. Whitfield wanted her pastor to mention Mr. Whitfield in the morning's prayers. Her husband had joined the Navy and was presently serving His Majesty, the King.

The lady sent a handwritten message to the pulpit: "Timothy Whitfield, having gone to sea, his wife desires the prayers of the congregation for his safety."

The aging preacher, however, had trouble reading the scrawled note. Without thinking, he quickly pronounced:

"Timothy Whitfield, having gone to see his wife, desires the prayers of the congregation for his safety."

⊚   ⊚   ⊚

The England Winger carefully explained to the rest of his rugby team that in a line-out he will shout a name beginning with "e" if it's a short ball, and a name beginning with "o" if it's a long ball. At the first line-out the team heard him shouting, "Oedipus!"

⊚   ⊚   ⊚

A young man was about to be married, but it wasn't until the night before the wedding that he tried on his suit. The rest of the family were horrified to see that the trousers were three inches too long. But the young man declared he couldn't care less, went to bed and fell fast asleep.

At about midnight, his sister was wide awake, worrying. So she sneaked into his room, cut three inches off the trouser legs, hemmed them up neatly and went back to bed satisfied.

At three in the morning, his mother, who hadn't slept a wink, got up, slipped into her son's room, and took three inches off the trouser legs. She hemmed them up, then crept quietly back to bed again.

At six in the morning, Grandma was up bright and early; she took the chance while her grandson was asleep to go quietly into his room, take three inches off the wedding trousers, and . . .

Communication Breakdown

One of the early Anglican charismatics, Michael Harper, was introduced on American TV as "the Anglican leader of the cosmetic revival"!

◎   ◎   ◎

And God said to Noah: "Will you build me an ark?"

"Yes, Lord. You know that I will. But there's just one question, Lord."

"Yes, Noah?"

"What's an ark?"

◎   ◎   ◎

Signing the register at a wedding, the best man had difficulty in making his ballpoint pen work. "Put your weight on it," said the vicar. He duly signed: "John Smith (ten stone, four pounds)."

◎   ◎   ◎

A man went around to the tradesman's entrance of a big house and asked if they had any odd jobs that he could do. After a moment's thought, the owner said he would pay him

£25 to go around to the front of the house and paint the porch.

After only a couple of hours the man came back with the pot of white paint and declared that he had finished the job.

"That was very quick!" exclaimed the owner.

"Yes, well it's not all that big—and, by the way, it's a Mercedes, not a Porsche!"

Six-year-old Margaret asked her father when their new baby would talk. He told her that it would not be for two years, since little babies don't talk.

"Oh yes they do!" Margaret insisted. "Even in the Bible they do!"

"What makes you say that?" he asked.

"When the lady read the Bible this morning in church, she definitely said that Job cursed the day he was born!"

Conformity

He who marries the spirit of the age is sure to be a widower in the next.

G. K. Chesterton

We forfeit three-fourths of ourselves in order to be like other people.

Schopenhauer

Conversion

Conversion is an initial event which must become a continuous process, not something static and frozen, but a dynamic, ongoing success.

Bishop George Appleton

◎   ◎   ◎

Philosophers have only interpreted the world differently; the point is, however, to change it.

Karl Marx

◎   ◎   ◎

A converted cannibal is one who, on Fridays, eats only fishermen.

◎   ◎   ◎

Ten reasons why I never wash:

1. I was made to wash as a child.
2. People who wash are hypocrites—they reckon they're cleaner than other people.
3. There are so many different kinds of soap, I could never decide which one was right.
4. I used to wash, but it got boring, so I stopped.
5. I still wash on special occasions, like Christmas and Easter.
6. None of my friends wash.
7. I'm still young. When I'm older and have got a bit dirtier, I might start washing.
8. I really don't have time.
9. The bathroom's never warm enough.
10. People who make soap are only after your money.

Daft, isn't it? We all need to wash, and we know it. There's no argument!

And we all need a personal friendship with Jesus, too. The need may not be quite so obvious, but it's there all the same.

Jesus can do something soap and water can never do: he can make us clean *on the inside*! And that can't be bad!

Like to know how he does it? We'd be glad to explain—
without any flannel or soft soap!

Christian Publicity Organization, Worthing

◎   ◎   ◎

Two caterpillars were sitting on a cabbage leaf, looking up
at a beautiful butterfly, and one said to the other, "You'll
never get me up in one of those things!"

◎   ◎   ◎

Revolution transforms everything except the human heart.

Victor Hugo

◎   ◎   ◎

Why Communism failed: Communism decrees, "On every
man a new suit." Christianity says, "In every suit a new man."

Convictions

Give us clear vision that we may know where to stand and
what to stand for, because unless we stand for something,
we shall fall for anything.

Peter Marshall

Covering Your Tracks

A minister wrote: "Don't be surprised if you find mistakes in
this church newsletter. We print something for everyone.
And some people are always looking for mistakes."

Creation

Teacher: How did the universe come into being?

| Student: | I'm terribly sorry, sir; I'm sure I did know, but I'm afraid I've forgotten. |
| Teacher: | How very unfortunate. Only two persons have ever known how the universe came into being: the Author of Nature and yourself. Now one of the two has forgotten! |

Criticism

Horse Sense

A horse can't pull while kicking,
This fact we merely mention,
And he can't kick while pulling,
Which is our chief contention.

Let us imitate the good horse,
And lead a life that's fitting;
Just pull an honest load, and then
There'll be no time for kicking.

The Cross

Our hope lies not in the man we put on the moon, but in the man we put on the cross.

Don Basham

Cynicism

The cynic is one who never sees a good quality in a man, and never fails to see a bad one. He is the human owl, vigilant in darkness and blind to light, mousing for vermin and never seeing noble game. The cynic puts all human actions into two classes: openly bad and secretly bad.

Henry Ward Beecher

Death

My grandfather would look through the obituary columns and say to me, "Strange, isn't it, how everybody seems to die in alphabetical order?"

◎ ◎ ◎

I'm not afraid to die; I just don't want to be there when it happens.
Woody Allen

◎ ◎ ◎

I don't want to achieve immortality through my work; I want to achieve it by not dying.
Woody Allen

◎ ◎ ◎

Obviously one isn't indestructible—quite.
Margaret Thatcher, 1988

◎ ◎ ◎

Dr. Donald Grey Barnhouse told of the occasion when his first wife had died. He was driving his children home from the funeral service. Naturally, they were overcome with grief, and Dr. Barnhouse was trying hard to think of some word of comfort to give them. Just then, a huge truck passed them. As it did so, its shadow swept over the car; and as it passed on in front, an idea came to him.

"Children," he said, "would you rather be run over by a truck or by its shadow?" They replied, "The shadow, of course; that can't hurt us at all." So Dr. Barnhouse then said, "Did you know that two thousand years ago the truck of death ran over the Lord Jesus . . . in order that only its shadow might run over us?"

Denominations

A strict Baptist visiting Newmarket finds himself at the race course and, knowing that nobody knows him there, decides to have a flutter. He goes to the paddock first and is intrigued to see a Catholic priest praying in Latin over a horse. He is even more surprised when it wins. The priest prays over two or three more horses and they all win. So finally, the Baptist lays half the church funds on the horse the priest next prays over. The horse starts well but then keels over before the first fence. The Baptist is distraught and rushes to ask the priest what happened. "Ah, that's the trouble with you Baptists," the priest replies, "you don't know the difference between a blessing and the last rites!"

I don't mind the walls of denominationalism, but I object to the broken glass on top!

Anglicans:	Everything is prohibited, except that which is permitted.
Baptists:	Everything is permitted, except that which is prohibited.
Methodists:	Everything is permitted, even that which is prohibited.
Brethren:	Everything is prohibited, even that which is permitted.

(Vary the labels according to preference.)

For Baptists, "the priesthood of all believers" means that even the pope is sometimes right.

A man ran to stop another man from flinging himself off a bridge into a river.

"Why are you killing yourself?" he asked.

"I've nothing to live for!"

"Don't you believe in God?"

"Yes, I do."

"What a coincidence—so do I! Are you a Jew or a Christian?"

"A Christian."

"What a coincidence—so am I! Protestant or Catholic?"

"Protestant."

"What a coincidence—so am I! Anglican or Baptist?"

"Baptist."

"What a coincidence—so am I! Strict and Particular, or General?"

"Strict and Particular."

"What a coincidence—so am I! Premillennial or Amillennial?"

"Premillennial."

"What a coincidence—so am I! Partial rapture or Full rapture?"

"Partial rapture."

At this, the first man sprang on the second and pushed him into the river, shouting "Die, infidel!"

There was once a preacher, a Baptist and a staunch Baptist at that. No other denomination was really *Christian* in his view. If you weren't a Baptist—well, you were just the pits! He went to preach at a church that was preparing to take part in a week of prayer for Christian unity. At the end of the meeting he asked, "How many people in this church are Baptist?"

It was a Baptist church and, knowing his reputation, almost all the local non-Baptists had stayed away. So nearly everyone in the congregation put up their hands—all except one little old lady.

The preacher decided to embarrass her. He told the others to put their hands down and he said to her, "What denomination are you?"

"I'm a Methodist," she replied.

"A *what*?"

"A Methodist," she said.

"And *why* are you a Methodist?" he asked.

"Well," she said, "my father was a Methodist and my grandfather was a Methodist, so I'm a Methodist."

The preacher decided that he would really make his point here, so he said,

"That's simply ridiculous! Suppose your father was a moron and your grandfather was a moron, what would *that* make you?"

The little old lady thought for a moment, then replied,

"I guess that would make me a Baptist!"

◎　　◎　　◎

You serve God in your way, and we serve him in his.

◎　　◎　　◎

A Presbyterian, a Methodist and a Baptist were discussing which church Jesus would join if he were to return to earth.

"He would obviously join the Presbyterians," said the Presbyterian, "because we have the form of government nearest to the New Testament pattern."

"No," said the Methodist, "he would join *us* because of our emphasis on preaching and fellowship."

Eventually, they turned to the Baptist, who had been silent all this time. "And what do you think?" they asked.

He replied, "I don't see why he should want to transfer his membership!"

Depression

You can run from war,
You can run from the law,
You can run from the cop on the beat.
You can run from danger,

You can run from a stranger,
But you can't run away from your feet.

He was so low that he could sit on a cigarette paper and dangle his legs.

Diplomacy

. . . the art of letting someone else have your way.

Disappointment

On his first parachute jump the soldier receives instructions from his sergeant: "You count to ten and then pull this cord. If the parachute fails, you pull the emergency parachute cord here. And then try to land near the lorry down there—they will have a nice cup of tea waiting for you."

The parachutist counts to ten and pulls the cord. Nothing happens. He pulls the emergency cord. Nothing happens. As he hurtles towards the lorry, he is heard to mutter, "I bet there's no cup of tea, either!"

Discipleship

By blood and origin, I am all Albanian.
My citizenship is Indian.
I am a Catholic nun.
As to my calling, I belong to the whole world.
As to my heart, I belong entirely to Jesus.

Mother Teresa

Unused truth becomes as useless as an unused muscle.

A. W. Tozer

◎   ◎   ◎

Dietrich Bonhoeffer, one of the Christian martyrs of Germany under the Nazis, said, "Discipleship means allegiance to the suffering Christ."

Great leaders have always demanded personal allegiance. King Arthur bound his knights to him by rigid vows. Garibaldi, the nineteenth-century Italian patriot, offered his followers hunger, death—and Italy's freedom. Sir Winston Churchill's stirring speech in the House of Commons on 13 May 1940, is best remembered for his dramatic words: "I have nothing to offer but blood, toil, tears and sweat."

Discretion

. . . is raising one's eyebrows instead of the roof.

Disobedience

Disobedience, as well as obedience, has the power to transform a person completely. Through disobedience in a particular decision, one can falsify the whole sequence of right thinking. The pastoral epistles talk about this a lot.

Disobedience comes in a variety of disguises: as superficial indifference or as the continuous creation of problems; as ascetic rigorism or as sectarianism; as the quest for novelty or as a philosophical restlessness. All that stuff is given a lot of weight preeminently to cover a scar in the conscience that lies hidden in the background.

Dietrich Bonhoeffer

Dogma

Every dogma has its day.

Doublespeak

Dialogue at a dinner party full of showbiz personalities:
"And what are you doing at the moment?"
"I'm writing a book."
"Neither am I . . ."

Dreams

Some girls long for beauty
And others wish for fame;
Those that burn with ambition yearn
To carve in stone their name.

I have but one desire,
And there endeavor ends:
To get my hooks on all the books
That I have lent to friends.

Education/Unemployment

What are the first words of a doctoral graduate in his first job?
"Anything to go with the Big Mac and fries?"

Encouragement

It may be that you don't like your church's minister. Well, here
is a tested prescription by which you can get rid of him (or her):

1. Look him straight in the eye when he's preaching and maybe say "Amen" occasionally. He'll preach himself to death in a short time.
2. Start paying him whatever he's worth. Having been on starvation wages for years, he'll promptly eat himself to death.
3. Shake hands with him and tell him he's doing a good job. He'll work himself to death.
4. Rededicate your own life to God and ask the minister to give you some church work to do. Very likely he'll keel over with heart failure.
5. If all else fails, this one is certain to succeed: get your congregation to unite in prayer for him. He'll soon be so effective that some larger church will take him off your hands.

Eternity

The stars shine over the mountains,
  the stars shine over the sea.
The stars look up to the mighty God,
  the stars look down on me;
The stars shall last for a million years,
  a million years and a day.
But God and I will live and love
  when the stars have passed away.

Robert Louis Stevenson

Ethics

Twentieth-century ethics can be summed up as: Do unto others before they do you!

We have grasped the mystery of the atom, but we have rejected the Sermon on the Mount. We have achieved brilliance without wisdom and power without conscience. Ours is a world of nuclear giants and ethical infants.

Joseph R. Sizoo

Evangelism

A newly employed salesman stunned his bosses with his first written report, for it demonstrated quite clearly that he was nearly illiterate. He wrote, "I seen this outfit who aint never bought ten cents worth of nothin from us and sole them some goods. i am now going to Chicawgo." Before they could fire him, a second report arrived and it read, "I came to Checawgo an sole them haff a millyon." Hesitant to dismiss the man, yet afraid of what would happen if he didn't, the sales manager transferred the problem into the company president's lap.

The next day the staff were amazed to see the salesman's two reports on the bulletin board, with this memo from the president: "We ben spendin two much time tryin to spel insted of tryin to sel. I want everybody should read these letters from Gooch, who is doin a grate job, and you should go out and do like he done!"

Doug Barnett

When I enter that beautiful city,
and the saints all around me appear,
I hope that someone will tell me
It was *you* who invited me here.

Existentialism

Explaining how he did so well in his philosophy exam, Woody Allen said, "I didn't know any of the answers, so I left it all blank. I got 100 percent."

Experience

There are many things we need to see or experience for ourselves before really understanding them:

> "Bitzer," said Thomas Gradgrind, "your definition of a horse."
>
> "Quadruped. Gramnivorous. Forty teeth, namely twenty-four grinders, four eye-teeth, and twelve incisive. Sheds coat in the spring; in marshy countries sheds hoofs too. Hoofs hard, but requiring to be shod with iron. Age known by marks in mouth." Thus (and much more) Bitzer.
>
> "Now, girl number twenty," said Mr. Gradgrind, "you know what a horse is."
>
> Charles Dickens, in *Hard Times*

Extremes

A man fell asleep in his usual place in a commuter train. Somewhat unusually, the train stopped just short of the station, waiting for the signal to change. The man woke up with a start, sprang up, opened the carriage door, stepped out and fell onto the track. But he quickly climbed back in again. As he shut the door, he said to his fellow passengers, "I bet you think I'm really stupid!"

Then he walked across to the other door, opened it, and fell out onto the embankment.

Facts

Facts do not cease to exist because they are ignored!

Aldous Huxley

Faith

. . . is trying to believe what you know isn't true.

◎   ◎   ◎

. . . is sitting on a branch while the Devil is sawing through it and believing the tree will fall down!

◎　　◎　　◎

. . . and its opposite: stupidity

◎　　◎　　◎

Two friends were looking through a holiday brochure and decided to go on this incredibly cheap trip to the Caribbean. When the trip got underway, they weren't too surprised to find that the plane had very few modern amenities (it had only an outside bathroom), but they were more surprised when, somewhere over the Atlantic, the floor opened and they were dropped thousands of feet into the ocean. However, a liferaft was dropped down after them.

As they clambered in, one of them said to the other, "I suppose they *will* send help for us?"

The other replied, "Well, they didn't last year!"

◎　　◎　　◎

Three men were walking on a wall,
Feeling, Faith and Fact.
When Feeling got an awful fall,
Then Faith was taken back.
So close was Faith to Feeling,
That he stumbled and fell too,
But Fact remained and pulled Faith back,
And Faith brought Feeling too.

◎　　◎　　◎

God sent sex to drive a man to marriage, ambition to drive a man to service, and fear to drive a man to faith.

Martin Luther

Fame

If the Lord's going to raise you up, then he'll raise you up. But if he doesn't raise you up, then for God's sake don't *you* do it!

Families

> We have careful thought for the stranger
> And smiles for the sometime guest
> But oft for our own the bitter tone
> Though we love our own the best.
>
> Margaret E. Sangster

◎ ◎ ◎

The little lady of the house, by way of punishment for some minor misdemeanor, was compelled to eat her dinner alone at a small table in the corner of the dining room. The rest of the family paid no attention to her until they heard her saying grace: "I thank thee, Lord, for preparing a table before me in the presence of my enemies."

◎ ◎ ◎

> To our forefathers, our faith was an experience.
> To our fathers, our faith was an inheritance.
> To us, our faith is a convenience.
> To our children, our faith is a nuisance.

◎ ◎ ◎

Praying Samuels come from praying Hannahs . . . and praying leaders come from praying homes.

Edward M. Bounds

Fanaticism

A fanatic is someone who can't change his mind and won't change the subject.

Sir Winston Churchill

◎ ◎ ◎

God finds it easier to cool down a fanatic than to warm up a corpse.

George Verwer

Fighting Back

A church near the flight path of London's Heathrow Airport displays a cartoon of a Concorde flying past its steeple, with the air hostess telling the pilot, "The passengers are complaining about the noise of the singing, sir!"

Flattery

After a loquacious and flattering introduction by his host, the speaker prays, "Lord, forgive my brother for all the wonderful but exaggerated things he said about me, and forgive me for enjoying every word."

Follow-Up

An evangelist and a pastor took a holiday together to go bear hunting in Canada. One evening the pastor was sitting in their log cabin when he heard cries for help. Looking out of the window, he saw the evangelist rushing toward the hut, hotly pursued by a huge grizzly bear. The pastor jumped up to open the door to let his friend in, but at the last minute, the evangelist side-stepped the door while the bear plunged on in. As the evangelist pulled the door shut from the outside, he yelled, "You deal with that one—I'll go and get some more!"

Forgiveness

Always forgive your enemies—nothing annoys them so much.

Oscar Wilde

An Episcopal Church in the United States advertised what it had to offer: "In the church started by a man with six wives, forgiveness goes without saying."

Every saint has a past and every sinner has a future.

Oscar Wilde

When the Devil reminds you of your past, you remind him of his future!

One of the classic films of 1987 was *The Mission*. In it, a soldier, Captain Mendoza, kills his brother in a feud over a woman they both love. Afterward, desperately depressed and consumed by remorse, he feels that the only way to get rid of his burden of guilt and sin is to perform some sort of penance. So he ties a huge net to his back, fills it with boulders, and sets himself to climb a high mountain.

In the company of a priest and some others, he travels over bracken, gorse and rocks, across rivers and through forests. You see him, cut, bruised and bleeding, a broken figure, crawling up the mountainside, the huge weight dragging behind him. From time to time, the others in the group urge him to let go of the burden. "You don't have to carry it anymore," they say. But he cannot leave it.

Eventually, reaching the top of the mountain, he collapses, exhausted. And then a little boy comes up to him—and cuts the net from him. As the net and rocks cascade down the mountainside, Mendoza is filled with a feeling of total release; his burden is gone and he knows he has been forgiven.

Forgiveness / Catch 22!

We will not accept into our membership anyone unless he is an active, disciplined, working member in one of our organizations.

Lenin

Freedom

Because of Christ, this wheelchair has become the prison that set me free.

Joni Eareckson Tada

◎　　◎　　◎

There are two kinds of freedom: the false, when a man is free to do what he likes; the true, when a man is free to do what he ought.

Charles Kingsley

Fulfillment

I may, I suppose, regard myself, or pass for being, a relatively successful man. People occasionally stare at me in the streets—that's fame. I can fairly easily earn enough to qualify for admission to the higher slopes of the Inland Revenue—that's success. Furnished with money and a little fame, even the elderly, if they care to, may partake of trendy diversion—that's pleasure. It might happen once in a while that something I said or wrote was sufficiently heeded for me to persuade myself that it represented a serious impact on our time—that's fulfillment.

Yet I say to you—and I beg you to believe me—multiply these tiny triumphs by a million, add them all together, and they are nothing—less than nothing, a positive impediment—measured against one draught of that living water Christ offers to the spiritually thirsty, irrespective of who or what they are.

Malcolm Muggeridge

Genius

In the Republic of Mediocrity, genius is dangerous.

Robert Ingersoll

◎ ◎ ◎

Genius is the ability to reduce the complicated to the simple.

◎ ◎ ◎

True genius resides in the capacity for evaluation of uncertain, hazardous and conflicting information.

Sir Winston Churchill

◎ ◎ ◎

Paderewski, the Polish pianist, was once approached by a woman after one of his concerts. "Paderewski," she said, "you are a genius!"

"Yes, madam," he replied, "but for many years before that, I was a drudge."

Gifting

A dog goes into the local Job Center. The interviewer is a little nonplussed, but eventually sends him along to a circus that is in town.

Next day the dog is back again, and the Job Center man asks how he got on at the circus. "Oh, that was no good," replies the dog. "They wanted a performing dog and I'm a bricklayer."

Giving

Do your givin'
While you're livin'
Then you're knowin'
Where it's goin'!

God

It is much worse to have a false idea of God than no idea at all.

Archbishop William Temple

◎   ◎   ◎

A German general asked an English officer why the British always won the wars between them, though there was little difference in their forces.

"We pray to God before each battle," said the Englishman.

"But we do, too," the general replied.

"Surely," replied the Englishman, "you don't expect God to understand German, do you?"

Gossip

Alan Redpath once formed a small group for mutual encouragement and laid down a rule that would bar gossip:

"The members subscribed to a simple formula applied before speaking of any person or subject that was perhaps controversial:

T - Is it true?

H - Is it helpful?

I - Is it inspiring?

N - Is it necessary?

K - Is it kind?

If what I am about to say does not pass those tests, I will keep my mouth shut! And it worked!"

from *A Passion for Preaching*

Grace

A preacher's small son had to apologize for forgetting his aunt's birthday. He wrote,

"I'm sorry I forgot your birthday. I have no excuse, and it would serve me right if you forgot mine, which is next Friday."

The Grand Highway?

Sound theology

Prone to heresy

Roof repairs in progress

Organ requires tuning

Disagreement among members

St. John's Bitton, North Yorkshire

Gratitude

In Ogden Nash's poem, *The Outcome of Mr. MacLeod's Gratitude*, he tells of a wife who was always complaining and a husband who managed to be grateful for everything. The last stanza runs:

> So she tired of her husband's cheery note
> And she stuffed a tea-tray down his throat.
> He remarked from the floor, where they found him reclining,
> "I'm just a MacLeod with a silver lining!"

A farmer was showing a man around his farm one day when they came to the pigsty—and there was a magnificent pig with a wooden leg. Not surprisingly, the visitor asked about the wooden leg.

The farmer replied, "Arr . . . now that's a very special pig. One night when we were all in bed, the farm caught fire. But that pig saw it, broke out of the sty, called the fire brigade, threw buckets of water on the fire, then rushed into the farmhouse and rescued me, my wife and the children. Yes, that's a very special pig!"

"And did he lose his leg trying to fight the fire?" inquired the visitor.

"Oh, no! But a very special pig like that—you don't eat it all at once!"

Guidance

Woman to man digging a hole in the road: "How do you get to the Royal Albert Hall?"

"Lady, you have to practice!"

Policeman to driver going the wrong way up a one-way street: "Didn't you see the arrows?"

Driver: "I didn't even see the Indians!"

Guilt

Man is the only animal who blushes—or needs to!

Mark Twain

Healing

An advertisement in the *Southport Visitor* read: "A healing session by John Cain (of Birkenhead): Owing to illness: meeting cancelled."

Peterborough, *Daily Telegraph*

Heaven

In our present condition the joys of heaven would be an acquired taste.

C. S. Lewis

◎　◎　◎

Heaven is not just "pie in the sky by and by"; it's "steak on the plate while you wait"!

◎　◎　◎

A couple about to get married are killed in a car crash and end up at the Pearly Gates the day before their wedding would have taken place. They mention to St. Peter that they would like a minister to marry them as soon as it is convenient. He says this will be no problem, but one hundred years later, when nothing has happened, they dare to ask him again if he could arrange the ceremony. "I'm so sorry," he replies, "we're still waiting for a minister!"

Hell

> Hell is oneself;
> Hell is alone, the other figures in it
> merely projections. There is nothing to escape from
> And nothing to escape to. One is always alone.
>
> T. S. Eliot, *The Cocktail Party*

Hindrances

A hindrance is someone who gets things off to a flying stop.

Homelessness

An article in the *Independent* newspaper in December 1992 quoted the following statistics:

"More than 600 homeless people died on the streets of England and Wales [in 1991] . . . Based on coroners' records, it shows death rates among homeless people are three times higher than for the rest of the population. The homeless are also:

- 150 times more likely to be killed in an assault;
- Thirty-four times more likely to kill themselves;
- Eight times more likely to die of an accident;
- Three times more likely to die of pneumonia.

. . . The average age of death was forty-seven, compared with an average life expectancy in Britain of seventy-three for men and seventy-nine for women."

Honesty

The children in a prominent family decided to give their father a book of the family's history for a birthday present. They commissioned a professional biographer to do the work, carefully warning him of the family's "black sheep" problem: Uncle George had been executed in the electric chair for murder.

"I can handle that situation so that there will be no embarrassment," the biographer assured the children. "I'll merely say that Uncle George occupied a chair of applied electronics at an important Government Institution. He was attached to his position by the strongest ties, and his death came as a real shock."

The Hollywood film director, Sam Goldwyn, said:

"I don't want any 'yes-men' around me. I want men and women who tell me the truth, even it if costs them their jobs!"

Hope (False)

Probably nothing in the world arouses more false hope than the first four hours of a diet.

Human Beings

Such is the human race. Often it does seem such a pity that Noah . . . didn't miss the boat.

Mark Twain

Humility

The *Church Times* recalls a story about the late Dr. Newport White when he was Regius Professor of Divinity at Dublin. On one great occasion somebody noticed him sitting unrobed in a pew and whispered, "Shouldn't you be in the procession?" To which the worthy Doctor replied, "Just a little ostentatious humility."

During the prayers in the vestry before the service, the deacon prayed: "Lord, take our preacher this evening and just blot him out."

A Keswick speaker started his address with the comment, "You know, you only get to speak at Keswick twice: once on your way up, and once on your way down. It's nice to be back again!"

Corrie ten Boom was once asked if it was difficult for her to remain humble. Her reply was this:
    "When Jesus rode into Jerusalem on Palm Sunday on the back of a donkey, and everyone was waving palm branches

and throwing garments on the road and singing praises, do you think that for one moment it ever entered the head of that donkey that any of that was for him?"

She continued, "If I can be the donkey on which Jesus Christ rides in his glory, I give him all the praise and all the honor."

After a long introduction to a speaker, which listed all his outstanding achievements, the speaker stood up and said, "I feel like the fly that hit the windshield; I never knew I had so much in me!"

Humor

Will Rogers, the American humorist, commented that "Everything is funny as long as it is happening to somebody else."

O Lord, make my enemies ridiculous!

Voltaire

Wit is a sword; it is meant to make people feel the point as well as see it.

G. K. Chesterton

Hypocrisy

The Eastern European theologian Dr. Peter Kusmic writes, "A credible message needs a credible messenger because charisma without character is catastrophe!"

◎　　◎　　◎

He was a good man in the worst sense of the term.

Mark Twain

◎　　◎　　◎

There are only two things I can't stand about him: his face.

◎　　◎　　◎

A lion met a tiger
  as they drew beside a pool.
Said the tiger, "Tell me why
  you're roaring like a fool."
"That's not foolish," said the lion
  with a twinkle in his eyes.
"They call me king of all the beasts
  because I advertise!"
A rabbit heard them talking
  and ran home like a streak.
He thought he'd try the lion's plan
  but his roar was just a squeak.
A fox came to investigate—
  had luncheon in the woods;
So when you advertise, my friend,
  be sure you've got the goods!

◎　　◎　　◎

The number one cause of atheism is Christians. Those who proclaim God with their mouths and deny him with their lifestyles is what an unbelieving world finds simply unbelievable.

Karl Rahner

◎　　◎　　◎

A vicar was asked to take the funeral for a non-church-going parishioner. "We want a nice Christian funeral," the family said, "but nothing religious."

Idealism

An idealist is a man with both feet planted firmly in the air.

Franklin D. Roosevelt

Identity

A group of British soldiers got lost in the desert during the Gulf War. They eventually stumbled across an American Five-Star General who was surveying the field. "Do you know where we are?" the men blurted out.

The General, very annoyed that they were improperly dressed, didn't salute or address him as "Sir," responded with an indignant question, "Do you know who I am?"

"Now we've got a real problem," said one of the soldiers. "We don't know where we are, and he doesn't know who he is!"

We have become a grandmother.

Margaret Thatcher, 4 March 1989

Immaturity

Out of the mouths of babes comes a lot of what they should have swallowed.

Franklin B. Jones

Incarnation

He became what we are that he might make us what he is.

Athanasius, fourth-century theologian and apologist

Inconsistency/Ups and Downs

A parachutist hurtles towards the ground, his parachute having failed to open. As he fumbles and panics, he is amazed to pass a man going up.

"Do you know anything about parachutes?" he shouts to him.

"No! Do you know anything about gas ovens?"

Indifference

They came first for the Communists, and I didn't speak up because I wasn't a Communist. Then they came for the Jews, and I didn't speak up because I wasn't a Jew. Then they came for the Trade Unionists, and I didn't speak up because I wasn't a Trade Unionist. Then they came for the Catholics, and I didn't speak up because I was a Protestant. Then they came for me—and there was no one left to speak up for me.

Martin Niemoller, German pastor,
victim of Nazi concentration camp

Inner City

A little boy was saying his prayers on the last night before his family moved from Devon: "Well, it's 'goodbye' from me, now, God—we're going to live in London."

Insincerity

He had a permanent SWEG—a Slimy Wet Evangelical Grin.

He was an Evangellyfish—he stung you with a gospel text and moved off smartly.

Integrity

Why is it that men know what is good but do what is bad?

Socrates

◎　◎　◎

What is morally wrong can never be politically right.

Abraham Lincoln

Intelligence

He was so clever that he didn't take a book to bed with him, he just browsed through his mind for half an hour.

Douglas Adams

Interlude

. . . to wake up the congregation.

◎　◎　◎

I've had a wonderful evening—but this wasn't it.

Groucho Marx

Involvement

Henry Dunant was born to wealthy parents in Switzerland in 1828. Deeply compassionate, he devoted considerable time to assisting and encouraging young people, especially the poor. When only about eighteen, he founded a Young Men's Christian Union.

Later, this sensitive person journeyed to Italy for an audience with Emperor Napoleon III, who was busy driving the

Austrians out of northern Italy. Arriving shortly after a horrendous battle, Henry Dunant couldn't believe what he saw. Some 40,000 men, wounded, dying and dead, lay scattered over a bloody terrain for vermin and vultures to consume.

Forgetting his personal agenda, Dunant pitched in, doing whatever he could to help the overworked doctors. He subsequently wrote and spoke on the horrors of war. At last the Geneva Convention of 1864 convened to consider common problems. Twenty-two nations took part and signed accords acknowledging the neutrality of medical personnel in time of hostility. They chose as their banner and symbol a red cross on a white field. And so the Red Cross was born.

Joy

I have tried in my time to be a philosopher; but, I don't know how, cheerfulness was always breaking in.

Samuel Johnson

Judgmentalism/Jumping to Conclusions

There were three zoology students, and each was sent to a different part of the world to find out about spiders.

The first was sent to Africa. After a few weeks, a report arrived for his professors, saying that he'd discovered some spiders that climbed trees.

The second student was sent to South America. After a few months, a posthumous report arrived saying that he'd discovered a lethal species of spider.

The third was sent to Australia. They heard not a word from him for a whole year, but then he came back in person, bringing with him a carton full of the particular species of spider that he'd been studying.

Very excitedly, he rang up his professors and got them all to meet him one morning. When they were all sitting around the table, the student put one of the spiders in the middle of it.

He looked hard at it, said, "Walk!" and it obediently walked around the table and came back to the middle. The student said to it again, "Walk!" and again the spider walked around the table and came back to the middle.

Then the student caught up the spider, and his professors watched aghast as he picked off its eight legs, one by one. Then he put it down again in the middle of the table.

He looked at it hard.

"Walk!" he said. Nothing happened.

"Walk!" he said again, more loudly. Still nothing happened.

"There!" he exclaimed. "That proves my theory! Spiders without legs are deaf!"

Justice

I'm not interested in the bloody system! Why has he no food? Why is he starving to death?

    Bob Geldof, interviewed about starvation in Africa, 1985

◎   ◎   ◎

Learning that her husband had betrayed her, Vera Czermak jumped out of her third-story window in Prague. The Czech newspaper, *Vicerni Prahi,* reported that Mrs. Czermak was recovering in the hospital, after landing on her husband, who was killed.

◎   ◎   ◎

As a boy, Woodrow Wilson worshipped his father, who was a church minister, and was overjoyed when the stern man would allow him to come along on visits through the parish.

Later, when he was President of the United States, Wilson laughingly recalled the time when his father had taken him to see a neighbor. Seeing the horse and buggy that had brought the minister and his son, the concerned neighbor wondered aloud, "Reverend, how is it that you're so thin and gaunt, while your horse is so fat and sleek?"

The Reverend began a modest reply, but before he could say two words, his outspoken son announced, to the parishioner's dismay, "Probably because my father feeds the horse, and the congregation feeds my father."

Knowledge

Nothing worth knowing can be understood by the mind.

Woody Allen

Leadership

Lead, follow, or get out of the way!

Ted Turner, media mogul and owner of CNN

Leisure

Personally, I have always looked on cricket as organized loafing.

Archibishop William Temple

Lies

No man has a memory long enough to be a successful liar.

Abraham Lincoln

Life—Living a Worthwhile One

If you would not be forgotten
As soon as you're dead and rotten,

Either write things worth reading
Or do things worth the writing.
                                    Benjamin Franklin

◎   ◎   ◎

Life with Christ is an endless hope; without him, a hopeless end.

◎   ◎   ◎

May you live all the days of your life.
                                    Jonathan Swift

Life and the Spirit

The neatest, tidiest and most orderly place in town is usually the cemetery!

◎   ◎   ◎

Uncouth life is better than aesthetic death.

◎   ◎   ◎

Someone once asked Dwight Moody, the nineteenth-century American evangelist, "Have you been filled with the Holy Spirit?"
    "Yes," he replied, "but I leak!"

Listening

His thoughts were slow,
His words were few and never formed to glisten.
But he was a joy to all his friends,
You should have heard him listen!

Love

The biggest disease today is not leprosy or tuberculosis, but rather the feeling of being unwanted, uncared for and deserted by everybody. The greatest evil is the lack of love and charity.
                                    Mother Teresa

◎ ◎ ◎

Take away love and our earth is a tomb.

Robert Browning

◎ ◎ ◎

The Bible tells us to love our neighbors and also to love our enemies, probably because they are generally the same people.

G. K. Chesterton

◎ ◎ ◎

To live above with saints we love,
Oh! That will be glory!
To live below with saints we know,
Well, that's a different story!

Marriage

It is high time that our so-called experts on marriage, the family and the home, turned to the Bible. We have read newspaper columns and listened to counselors on the radio and TV; psychiatrists have had a land-office business. In it all, the One who performed the first marriage in the Garden of Eden and instituted the union between man and wife has been left out.

Billy Graham

◎ ◎ ◎

The greatest thing a man can do for his children is to love their mother.

Michael Cassidy

◎ ◎ ◎

Marriage: it starts when you sink into his arms and ends with your arms in his sink.

◎　◎　◎

The average wife would rather have beauty than brains, because she knows that the average husband can see better than he can think.

◎　◎　◎

To keep your marriage brimming
With love in the loving cup,
If ever you're wrong, admit it,
If ever you're right, shut up.

Ogden Nash

◎　◎　◎

Where the warfare is the hottest
In the battlefields of life,
You'll find the Christian soldier
Represented by his wife.

◎　◎　◎

A silly and childish game is one at which your wife can beat you.

◎　◎　◎

My wife and I were very happy for thirty years—and then we met!

◎　◎　◎

I love the human race. All of my family belong to it, and some of my husband's family, too.

◎　◎　◎

Marriage is a woman's way of calling a meeting to order.

Materialism

Let's stop loving things and using people, and start using things and loving people.

Meaning of Life

Mark Twain, whose literature has been enjoyed by many, became morose and weary of life. Shortly before his death, he wrote: "A myriad of men are born; they labor and sweat and struggle . . . they squabble and scold and fight; they scramble for little mean advantages over each other; age creeps upon them; infirmities follow . . . those they love are taken from them, and the joy of life is turned to aching grief. It [release] comes at last—the only unpoisoned gift earth had ever had for them—and they vanish from a world where they were of no consequence . . . a world which will lament them a day and forget them forever."

Media

Released in the United States in 1979 by Warner Brothers, the film *Jesus* has been dubbed into more than 130 languages and viewed in 155 countries by more than 355 million people. More than 200 mission agencies and denominations have used the film. By 1993, Campus Crusade, the catalyst for the translation effort, hopes to translate the film into all of the 271 languages spoken by more than one million people. Other organizations are interested in translating it into still more languages. Campus Crusade estimates that more than 30 million people have indicated decisions to follow Christ as a result of watching the film.

◎   ◎   ◎

Television is . . . a medium. So called because it is neither rare nor well done!

Ernie Kovacs

◎   ◎   ◎

I find television very educating. Every time somebody turns on the set, I go into the other room and read a book.

Groucho Marx

Meekness

Seen on a church noticeboard: "The meek will inherit the earth—if that's all right with you."

Ministers of Religion

Why don't ministers look out of their windows in the morning? Because they'd have nothing to do in the afternoon.

Miracles

Flying his private plane over Los Angeles, an eighty-year old pilot had a sudden heart attack and died at the controls. Without a moment's hesitation, the passenger, sixty-nine year old Charles Law—who had never flown a plane before— took over the wheel of the Cessna 150 and landed it safely at Upland, California. "I don't know how he did it," said police sergeant John Cameron, who led a convoy of ambulances and fire engines to the airstrip. "It was a miracle."

It certainly was. After he had landed, Charles Law had to be led gently from the plane. He is blind.

Perrott Philips in *Time Off* magazine

Misunderstanding

A man found a penguin wandering down the street, so took hold of its flipper and found the nearest policeman. "What shall I do with it?" he asked. The policeman thought for a moment and then suggested, "Take it around the corner to the zoo."

The next day the policeman bumped into the man again, still clutching the penguin by the flipper. Before the policeman could say anything, the man smiled and said, "Thanks for the idea about going to the zoo yesterday. I'm taking it to the pictures today!"

◎　◎　◎

A chaplain was asked to visit an oriental patient in intensive care. He soon discovered that the man didn't speak English, but as he stood and held his hand, the man constantly repeated a strange-sounding phrase. The man became more and more anguished until finally he passed away, still muttering those words.

The chaplain rang up a friend who came from the east, and asked him what the phrase meant. "Was it some last act of repentance?" he suggested.

"No," said the friend, "it simply means, 'You're standing on my oxygen supply.'"

◎　◎　◎

A Welsh preacher worked himself into a frenzy preaching on Psalm 42, "As the hart pants for the waterbrook, so longs my soul after Thee."

As he continued, he cried, "Yes, brothers and sisters! It's your pants he wants!"

Modesty

Church member to minister after the service: "You were really good this morning!"

Modestly, the minister replies, "Oh, it wasn't me; it was the Lord."

Church member: "You weren't *that* good!"

Money

The average English cat costs £145 per year to feed—which is more than the average income of the one billion people who live in the world's fifteen poorest nations.

◎   ◎   ◎

The trouble is that there's always too much month left at the end of the money.

◎   ◎   ◎

No one would have remembered the Good Samaritan if he'd only had good intentions. He had money as well.

Margaret Thatcher, speech, 1980

◎   ◎   ◎

No man is rich enough to buy back his past.

◎   ◎   ◎

Sometimes, when you've read through a long, spiritual prayer letter, you eventually realize that it was a veiled plea for more money. Those sorts of letters demonstrate that "faith without hints is dead."

◎   ◎   ◎

A pastor was driving back from a speaking engagement and decided to stop overnight in a motel. She pulled off the highway and went into the reception area of a nice-looking motel. "How much is a room for the night?" she asked.

"It's £110," replied the receptionist.

"Oh. Haven't you anything cheaper?"

"Well," said the receptionist, "it's £110 on the first floor but it's only £100 on the second floor."

"No, that's still too much," said the pastor.

"The third floor is £80," said the receptionist, helpfully.

"And what about the fourth?" asked the pastor.

"That's the top floor and that's £50 per night."

At that the pastor turned to go. "I'm sorry," she said, "your hotel just isn't tall enough for my pocket."

◎   ◎   ◎

From a church bulletin: "A number of buttons have been found among the coins in recent collections. In future, please rend your hearts and not your garments."

◎   ◎   ◎

As the parishioners were leaving church after a service, one woman said, in a loud voice, "I've nothing but praise for the new vicar!" A rather glum old usher who was passing by overheard her and remarked, "So I noticed when I passed you the collection bag."

Musical Misquotes

"I will make you vicious old men . . ."

◎   ◎   ◎

"Grind us together, Lord . . ."

◎   ◎   ◎

A little girl had a teddy bear with a lazy eye. She called it "Gladly," because she had sung about it in church: "Gladly my cross-eyed bear. . ."

New Age

I was caught cheating in a metaphysics exam. I was looking into the soul of the boy next to me.

Woody Allen

Obedience

A group of American tourists were on a conducted tour of the House of Commons when a Labour Lord entered the central lobby, wearing his ceremonial garb. He wanted to catch the attention of Neil Kinnock, who was over on the far side of the House, so he shouted, "Neil!" And fifty Americans dutifully knelt.

It's hard to get your heart and your head to agree in life. In my case, they're not even friendly.

Woody Allen

Optimism/Pessimism

'Twixt optimist and pessimist
The difference is droll:
The optimist sees the doughnut,
The pessimist sees the hole.

An optimist? The woman who slips her feet back into her shoes when the preacher says, "And finally . . ."

Just because you occasionally feel fed up, don't despair! Remember that the sun has a "sinking spell" every night but rises again in the morning.

◎   ◎   ◎

A couple have twin sons, one of whom is a pessimist and the other an optimist. The parents decide to try to even things out for their birthday, so they give the pessimist a marvellous hi-fi system. When he unwraps it, he complains, "With the price of CDs I'll never be able to afford any! And these things are always going wrong! And you'll soon be moaning about the noise . . ."

The optimist receives just a bag of horse manure. As he unwraps it, he leaps in the air with joy, crying, "There's a pony on its way!"

Originality

There is no such thing as an original joke.

Stephen Gaukroger and Nick Mercer

◎   ◎   ◎

I fear I have nothing original in me—excepting original sin.

Thomas Campbell

◎   ◎   ◎

Originality is the art of concealing your source.

Franklin Jones

Pastors

Nehemiah was the model pastor, dealing so gently with those who let their children marry outside the faith:

"So I argued with these parents and cursed them and punched a few of them and knocked them around and pulled out their hair; and they vowed before God that they would not let their children intermarry with non-Jews."

Nehemiah 13:25, The Living Bible

◎   ◎   ◎

The evangelist's job is to get people out of Egypt. The pastor's job is to get Egypt out of the people.

◎   ◎   ◎

The task of pastoral ministry is, above all else, to arrange the contingencies for an encounter with the Divine.

Dietrich Bonhoeffer

◎   ◎   ◎

Pastor, Priest, Vicar, Minister and friend . . .
whatever we call him or her, it's still a tough job:

If he visits his flock, he's nosey.
If he doesn't, he's a snob.
If he preaches longer than ten minutes, it's too long.
If he preaches less than ten minutes, he can't have prepared his sermon.
If he runs a car, he's worldly.
If he doesn't, he's always late for appointments.
If he tells a joke, he's flippant.
If he doesn't, he's far too serious.
If he starts the service on time, his watch must be fast.
If he's a minute late, he's keeping the congregation waiting.
If he takes a holiday, he's never in the parish.
If he doesn't, he's a stick-in-the-mud.
If he runs a gala or bazaar, he's money mad.
If he doesn't, there's no social life in the parish.
If he has the church painted and redecorated, he's extravagant.
If he doesn't, the church is shabby.
If he's young, he's inexperienced.
If he's getting old, he ought to retire.

But . . .

When he dies, there's never been anyone like him!

Adapted from *Beda Review,* via *Catholic Herald*

◎   ◎   ◎

According to a writer in *Parson and Parish,* when churches seek a new minister, they expect "the strength of an eagle, the grace of a swan, the gentleness of a dove, the friendliness of a sparrow and the night hours of an owl . . . Then when they catch the bird, they expect him to live on the food of a canary."

◎   ◎   ◎

The Deacon's prayer: "Lord, send us a poor, humble minister. You keep him humble and we'll keep him poor."

◎   ◎   ◎

"What's a Deacon, Johnny?"

"You put it on a hill, and when the enemy comes, you set fire to it!"

◎   ◎   ◎

Pastor and Doctor

Mrs. Huff is up the miff tree
On a seat fixed good and firm;
And she'd like to tell the pastor
A few things to make him squirm.

Mrs. Huff was sick abed, sir,
Yes, sir, sick abed a week!
And the pastor didn't call, sir,
Never even took a peek.

When I asked her if the doctor
Called to see her, she said, "Sure!"

And she looked as if she thought I
Needed some good mental cure.

Then I asked her how the doctor
Knew that sickness laid her low,
And she said that she had called him
On the phone and told him so.

Now the doctor gets his bill paid
With a nicely written cheque;
But the pastor, for not knowing,
Simply gets it in the neck.

◎   ◎   ◎

How many pastors does it take to change a light bulb?
Only one—but the bulb has really got to want to change.

◎   ◎   ◎

Two Yorkshire farmers were discussing their respective clerics. One said: "Our fellow's got foot and mouth disease. 'E don't visit and 'e can't preach!"

◎   ◎   ◎

A minister's job is to comfort the afflicted and to afflict the comfortable!

◎   ◎   ◎

A new shorthand code for churches trying to decide what sort of minister they are looking for:
A YUMMY: A young upwardly mobile minister.
A MUMMY: A middle-aged upwardly mobile minister.
A GUMMY: A geriatric upwardly mobile minister.

Permissiveness

We cannot have permissiveness in sex and expect that we will not also have permissiveness in violence, or in tax avoidance, or corruption and bribery in high places. People today want permissiveness in the bedroom, but not in the board rooms; in the casino, but not in the bank. If we promote permissiveness where we want it, we find permissiveness where we do not want it.

Sir Frederick Catherwood

Persistence

I am extraordinarily patient, provided I get my own way in the end.

Margaret Thatcher, quoted in *The Observer*, January 1983

◎   ◎   ◎

I've been knocked down, kicked around,
Some people scandalize my name,
But here I am, talking about Jesus just the same.
I've been knocked down, kicked around,
But like a moth drawn to the flame,
Here I am, talking about Jesus just the same.

Larry Norman

◎   ◎   ◎

If you're ever tempted to give up, just think of Brahms. He took seven years to compose his famous lullaby—he kept falling asleep at the piano!

Robert Orben

◎   ◎   ◎

By perseverance the snail reached the Ark.

Spurgeon

◎   ◎   ◎

Consider the postage stamp: its usefulness consists in the ability to stick to one thing until it gets there.

Josh Billings

◎   ◎   ◎

Seen on the side of an ice cream van: "Often licked but never beaten!"

◎   ◎   ◎

Frogs in Cream

Two frogs fell into a can of cream,
Or so I've heard it told;
The sides of the can were shiny and steep,
The cream was deep and cold.

"Oh, what's the use?" croaked Number 1,
"Tis fate; no help's around.
Goodbye, my friends! Goodbye, sad world!"
And, weeping still, he drowned.

But Number 2, of sterner stuff,
Dog-paddled in surprise,
The while he wiped his creamy face
And dried his creamy eyes.

"I'll swim awhile, at least," he said,
Or so I've heard he said;
"It really wouldn't help the world
If one more frog were dead."

An hour or two he kicked and swam,
Not once he stopped to mutter;
But kicked and kicked and swam and kicked,
then hopped out, via butter!

T. C. Hamlet

Personal Touch

Here is a love story. A young man and a young woman were deeply in love, and while he was away with the Navy for three years, he wrote to her every day, without fail. At the end of the three years came the happy wedding—she married the postman.

Personality

A well-balanced person? Someone who has a chip on both shoulders.

◎　　◎　　◎

As the little girl prayed: "Dear God, please make all the bad people good, and please make all the good people nice."

◎　　◎　　◎

Custard Christians: those who get upset over trifles.
Yogurt Christians: those who sour everything they mix with.

Pessimism

A pessimist is the person who looks through the obituary column in the newspaper to see if his name is there yet.

Pluralism

I think I need to pray; know any good religions?

Douglas Adams

◎　　◎　　◎

All roads may lead to Rome, but only one ends up in heaven.

Mark Green

Politically Correct Speech

Cerebrally non-motivated (stupid)
Chronologically gifted (old)
Differently sized (fat)
Follicularly challenged (bald)
Knowledgeably dispossessed (mistaken)
Hesychastic truths perceived through ontological media
    (certainty)
Atonally exciting (off-key)

Politics

Capitalism is man's exploitation of man, whereas communism is the exact opposite.

Pornography

At present the pornography industry in the UK is worth at least £500 million a year. In the United States it grosses more than the music and film industries combined.

Campaign Against Pornography and Censorship

Potential

One can count the number of seeds in an apple, but one cannot count the number of apples in a seed.

Llandridod Wells Church magazine

Poverty

When you're down and out, something always turns up—and it's usually the noses of your friends.

Orson Welles

Power

Of all forces, violence is the weakest.

Gobineau

Praise

Praise undeserved is satire in disguise.

The most obvious fact about praise—whether of God or anything—strangely escaped me . . . I had not noticed how the humblest, and at the same time most balanced and capacious minds, praised most, while the cranks, misfits and malcontents praised least. The good critics found something to praise in many imperfect works; the bad ones continually narrowed down the list . . . The healthy and unaffected man, even if luxuriously brought up and widely experienced in good cookery, could praise a very modest meal . . . the snob found fault with all . . . Praise almost seems to be inner health made audible.

C. S. Lewis

Prayer

I can concentrate better when my knees are bent.

A mother overheard her young son praying one day: ". . . and if you give me a bike, Lord, then I'll be good for a whole week."

She interrupted him and said, "Now, Johnny, it's no good trying to bargain with God. He won't answer prayers like that!"

A few days later she overheard him praying again: "... and if you give me a new bike, Lord, I'll be good for *three* weeks!"

"Johnny," said his mother gently, "I thought I told you it was no good trying to strike bargains with the Lord. He doesn't respond to that sort of prayer."

A few days later the mother was cleaning the house and, to her amazement, found right at the bottom of the airing cupboard, a little statue of the madonna that had stood on the sideboard. She guessed that this must be something to do with Johnny and went up to his room to find him. He wasn't there, but on the windowsill she found a note that read: "OK, Lord, if you ever want to see your mother again ...!"

Heard at the prayer meeting: "Lord, it was such a fantastic meeting last Saturday! All the things that happened and the 'words' we got ... You should've been there, Lord!"

The nineteenth-century Baptist preacher Charles Spurgeon was once asked, "When should I pray? Should I pray when I don't feel like it?"

He replied, "Pray when you feel like it, because God will bless you; pray when you don't feel like it, because that is when you need it most."

You probably remember playing with iron filings at school. You run a magnet over a bunch of iron filings and they all stand to attention or move to the right or to the left. Long before the magnet makes physical contact with the filings, something is happening. Why? Because an invisible power, magnetism, is affecting them.

In the same way, prayer, which is invisible and spiritual, affects that which is visible and physical.

Prayer and Action

A priest in a poor inner city area desperately needed money for a new church building. At his wits' end, he pleaded with God: "Lord, if you love me, let me win the national lottery this week!" Friday was the grand draw, but there was nothing for the priest.

He went back to church to plead with God again: "Lord, if you love me, let me win the national lottery this week!" But at the end of the week, another winner was announced.

A third time he returned to pray at the altar: "Lord, if you love me, let me win the national lottery this week!" As he got up to go, a voice boomed from the heavens: "OK. But meet me halfway. This week, buy a lottery ticket!"

Prayers Answered

I asked God for strength, that I might achieve.
I was made weak, that I might learn humbly to obey.
I asked for health, that I might do greater things.
I was given infirmity, that I might do better things.
I asked for riches, that I might be happy.
I was given poverty, that I might be wise.
I asked for power, that I might have the praise of men.
I was given weakness, that I might feel the need of God.
I asked for all things that I might enjoy life,
I was given life that I might enjoy all things.
I got nothing that I asked for—but everything that I had
    hoped for.
Almost, despite myself, my unspoken prayers were
    answered.
I am among all men, most richly blessed.

Anonymous Confederate soldier

Preachers and Preaching

Some students never study but, like the spider, spin everything out from within, making beautiful webs that never last. Some are like ants that steal whatever they find, store it away, and use it later. But the bee sets the example for us all. He takes from many flowers but he makes his own honey.

Francis Bacon

◎　◎　◎

My preacher's eyes I've never seen
Though the light in them may shine,
For when he prays, he closes his,
And when he preaches, I close mine.

◎　◎　◎

The vicar was hoping to get a discount on the price of a suit.
"I'm just a poor preacher!" he said to the shopkeeper.
"Yes, I know," the shopkeeper replied. "I've heard you preach."

◎　◎　◎

A rather timid minister was told by one part of the congregation to preach "the old-fashioned gospel," and by the rest to be more broadminded. One day he got up to preach and ended up saying, "Unless you repent, in a measure, and are saved, so to speak, you are, I am sorry to say, in danger of hellfire and damnation, to a certain extent."

◎　◎　◎

Now I lay me down to sleep:
The sermon's long and the subject deep;
If he gets through before I wake,
Someone give me a gentle shake.

◎　◎　◎

On accepting his first church, a young pastor asked an elderly board member if he had any wise advice. The elderly man responded, "Son, a sermon is like a good meal; you should end it just before we have had enough."

Preachers can talk
But never teach
Unless they practice
What they preach.

I preached as never sure to preach again, and as a dying man to dying men.

Richard Baxter

Orators are most vehement when their cause is weak.

Cicero

On the frequent lack of application of the text to life: We often speak eloquently of the general state of the rubber industry in the West, when people simply want to know how to mend a flat tire!

Bishop Festo Kivengere told the story of how he was going off to preach after a row with his wife. The Holy Spirit said to him, "Go back and pray with your wife!"

He argued, "I'm due to preach in twenty minutes. I'll do it afterwards."

"OK," said the Holy Spirit. "You go and preach; I'll stay with your wife."

"My lips are hermeneutically sealed."

◎   ◎   ◎

Well, the minister got to know a *little* Greek and Hebrew while he was at college. The Greek ran the kebab shop and the Hebrew made his suits!

◎   ◎   ◎

His preaching cost nothing—and it was worth it!

Mark Twain

◎   ◎   ◎

Little girl to her mummy: "Mummy, why does the pastor pray before his sermon?"

She replied, "He's asking God to help him preach a good sermon."

"Mummy, why doesn't God answer his prayer?"

Predictability

The British won't fight.

Leopoldo Galtieri to Alexander Haig, 10 April 1982

Preparedness

An unemployed actor finally landed a one-line part in a big West End play. He only had five words to say: "Hark! How the cannons roar!" and spent all his time practicing different ways of saying it.

On the morning of the first day of the performance, he ate his breakfast, muttering, "Hark! How the cannons roar!" As he caught the tube into the city he repeated to himself, "Hark! How the cannons roar!" Finally, as he stood in the wings waiting for his moment to come, he said over and over, "Hark! How the cannons roar!"

At last the moment came. He walked on stage and his cue came, "Bang!"

"What was that!?" he cried.

Principles

When a man approves of something in principle, it means he hasn't the slightest intention of putting it into practice.

Bismarck

A snippet in a national paper read: "A trustee of the British Vegetarian Society and a member of its National Council has resigned after he was found selling beefburgers at his village store at Tollerton near York."

A case of principles suspended for personal financial reasons?

Procrastination

The Devil doesn't care how much good we do, as long as we don't do it today.

Procrastination is my sin,
It brings me naught but sorrow.
I know that I should stop it,
In fact, I will—tomorrow!

Gloria Pitzer

Why put off till tomorrow what you can safely put off till the week after next?

Promises

Many people have seen the Passion Play performed in the Bavarian village of Oberammergau. It is a once-in-a-decade spectacular involving practically all 4,800 villagers and much of their livestock. The 1984 presentation marked its three hundred and fiftieth staging, and the eight-hour performance ran for one hundred days, beginning on May 20.

The tradition is said to have originated in 1633 when the survival of the village was threatened by plague. Its records for 1632 reveal that at least eighty-four villagers died from plague that year, and in 1633 they sought relief by promising God that if he would turn the plague away from them they would stage, every ten years, a drama reenacting the life and death of Christ. It is said that from that day the plague did not claim a single life in the community.

The following year, 1634, the villagers made good their promise and staged the first Passion Play.

Prophecy

H. L. Mencken, an American journalist covering a rather dull and, he thought, predictable presidential convention meeting, sent the press release the day before. However, a crucial issue in the meeting went quite the other way from what was expected. Mencken cabled the newspaper office with the simple instruction: "Insert 'not' as sense requires."

Prophecy (False)

Thus says the Lord: "I have nothing against you . . . as far as I know . . ."

Purpose

God has created me
to do him some definite service.
He has committed some work to me which he has
not
committed to another.
I have my mission.
I may never know it in this life,
but I shall be told it in the next.
I am a link in a chain,
a bond of connection between persons.
He has not created me for naught;
I shall do good—I shall do his work;
I shall be an angel of peace,
a preacher of truth in my own place
while not intending it
if I do but keep his commandments.
Therefore I will trust him.
Whatever I am, I can never be thrown away.
If I am in sickness, my sickness may serve him;
in perplexity, my perplexity may serve him.
If I am in sorrow, my sorrow may serve him.
He does nothing in vain.
He knows what he is about.
He may take away my friends,
he may throw me among strangers,
he may make me feel desolate,
make my spirits sink,
hide my future from me—still
He knows what he is about.

Cardinal Newman

Quarrels

People generally quarrel because they cannot argue.

G. K. Chesterton

Rebellion

A father repeatedly told his little boy to sit down on the back seat of the car. He remained standing until eventually, exasperated, the father physically sat the boy down.

The little boy grimaced and muttered, "I may be sitting down on the outside, but I'm standing up on the inside!"

Relationships

Bakker started out loving people and using things, but then he started loving things and using people.

> Jerry Miller, prosecutor at the fraud trial of Jim Bakker

Repentance

A deacon, frequently called on to pray at the church prayer meeting, always concluded his prayer, "And now, Lord, clean all the cobwebs out of our lives."

The others knew what he meant—all the little unsightly words, thoughts and deeds that we let accumulate in our lives. Finally it got too much for one of the brethren who had heard that prayer many times. So on hearing it again, he jumped to his feet and shouted, "Don't do it, Lord! Kill the spider!"

A painter not particularly noted for his honesty decided to water down the paint but charge his customer for the full amount he should have used. Unfortunately for him, he carried the process rather too far with the result that the finished work looked so bad that even the most shortsighted client would notice it.

"What can I do now?" he wailed.

From the heavens a great voice boomed, "Repaint! And thin no more!"

◎ ◎ ◎

A new Christian wrote to the Inland Revenue: "I can't sleep at night, so I am enclosing £100 I forgot to declare. P.S. If I still can't sleep, I will send the rest."

◎ ◎ ◎

Sleep with clean hands, either kept clean all day by integrity or washed clean at night by repentance.

John Donne

◎ ◎ ◎

It was bank holiday weekend, and a long queue had formed at the petrol station. When at last it was the vicar's turn, the attendant apologized for the long delay: "They knew they were going to make this trip, yet they all waited until the last minute to get ready!"

The vicar smiled ruefully. "I know what you mean," he said. "It's like that in my business, too!"

◎ ◎ ◎

Doctor to overweight patient: "Here's a list of what you must eat: lettuce, carrots, cabbage . . ."

"That's fine, doctor," interrupted the patient, "but do I take them before or after meals?"

Research

If you steal from one another, it's plagiarism. If you steal from many, it's research.

Responsibility

Young boy to his father, who is reading his appalling end-of-term report: "What do you think the trouble is, Dad? Heredity or environment?"

Restoration

In the former home of Sir Winston Churchill there is a large model of a ship. It is made out of thousands of discarded, burnt-out matches. All those finished, useless items have been patiently molded together and re-formed into something amazingly beautiful.

That's precisely what God wants to do with us. He wants to take the blackened embers of ruined lives, with all their failures and sin, and to create something beautiful and special for himself out of them. What seems bankrupt and useless to us is, to God, material to take up and turn into something special and glorious.

Risk-Taking

God equipped us with necks—we should occasionally stick them out!

If you don't go overboard, you tend not to make a splash.

Salvation

> Give me your tired, your poor,
> Your huddled masses yearning to breathe free,
> The wretched refuse of your teeming shore,
> Send these, the homeless, tempest-tossed, to me:
> I lift my lamp beside the golden door.
>
> Emma Lazarus

The Pit

A man fell into a pit and couldn't get himself out.

A *subjective* person came along and said, "I feel for you down there."

An *objective* person came along and said, "It's logical that someone would fall down there."

A *Pharisee* said, "Only bad people fall into pits."

A *news reporter* wanted the exclusive story on the man's pit.

Confucius said, "If you had listened to me, you wouldn't be in that pit."

Buddha said, "Your pit is only a state of mind."

A *realist* said, "That's a PIT."

A *scientist* calculated the pressure necessary (PSI) to get him out of the pit.

A *geologist* told him to appreciate the rock strata in the pit.

A *tax man* asked if he was paying taxes on the pit.

The *council inspector* asked if he had a permit to dig a pit.

An *evasive* person came along and avoided the subject of his pit altogether.

A *self-pitying* person said, "You haven't seen anything until you've seen MY pit!"

A *charismatic* said, "Just confess that you're not in a pit."

An *optimist* said, "Things could be worse."

A *pessimist* said, "Things will get worse."

Jesus, seeing the man, took him by the hand and lifted him out of the pit.

Kenneth D. Filkins

Salvation is moving from living death to deathless life.

Jack Odell

Second Coming of Christ

I've no idea when Jesus is coming back. I'm on the Welcoming Committee, not the Planning Committee.

Tony Campolo

Secularization

The first Law of Secularization: "Hollywood loves you and has a marvelous plan for your life."

Self-Pity

Self-pity is our worst enemy and, if we yield to it, we can never do anything wise in the world.

Helen Keller

Self-Sacrifice

The trouble with a living sacrifice is that it keeps crawling off the altar!

He is no fool who gives up what he cannot keep to gain what he can never lose.

Jim Elliot

Sermons

Several years ago the *British Weekly* printed a letter to the editor:

"Dear Sir,
   I notice that ministers seem to set a great deal of importance on their sermons and spend a great deal of time in preparing them. I have been attending services quite regularly for the past thirty years and during that time, if I estimate correctly, I have listened to no less than three thousand sermons. But, to my consternation, I discover I cannot

remember a single one of them. I wonder if a minister's time might be more profitably spent on something else?

Yours sincerely . . ."

That letter triggered an avalanche of angry responses for weeks. Sermons were castigated and defended by lay people and clergy, but eventually a single letter closed the debate:

"Dear Sir,

I have been married for thirty years. During that time I have eaten 32,000 meals—mostly of my wife's cooking. Suddenly, I have discovered that I cannot remember the menu of a single meal. And yet, I received nourishment from every one of them. I have the distinct impression that without them I would have starved to death long ago.

Yours sincerely . . ."

James Berkley

◎   ◎   ◎

A sermon doesn't have to be eternal to be immortal.

◎   ◎   ◎

A little boy in church asked his father, as the offering bags came around, "Daddy, what does that mean?"

"They're collecting our money for God."

As they knelt for prayer, the little boy asked, "Daddy, what does that mean?"

"It means we're talking to God."

And when the minister removed his watch at the start of the sermon, laying it in front of him on the pulpit, the little boy asked, "Daddy, what does that mean?"

"Absolutely nothing!"

◎   ◎   ◎

I don't mind people looking at their watches while I'm preaching, but I get worried when they take them off and shake them!

◎   ◎   ◎

I don't mind people looking at their watches when I preach, but it worries me when they get out their date books.

◎   ◎   ◎

One Sunday morning, the vicar apologized to his congregation for the band-aid on his face. "I was thinking about my sermon and cut my face," he said.

Afterward, in the collection plate, he found a note that read, "Next time, why not think about your face and cut the sermon?"

◎   ◎   ◎

A good sermon leaves you wondering how the preacher knew so much about you.

◎   ◎   ◎

A vicar about to speak at a formal dinner was announced by the MC with the words, "Pray for the silence of the Reverend Smith."

◎   ◎   ◎

After a rather long and dull sermon, the preacher asked a deacon, "Do you think I should have put more fire in my sermon?"

"You should have put more sermon in the fire!" he replied.

Service

No matter how humble our gifts, we can use them to serve God.

In 1963 the verger at Fairford Parish Church in Gloucestershire took pity on a stray kitten. It made its home in the church where it caught mice and scared off the bats.

Tiddles was well-behaved during sermons, usually sleeping through them, curled up on the lap of one of the congregation.

When it died, it was buried in the churchyard and a memorial was raised over the grave, recording seventeen years of faithful service as "The church cat."

◎   ◎   ◎

I don't know what your destiny will be, but one thing I know, the only ones among you who will be really happy are those who have sought and found how to serve.

Albert Schweitzer

◎   ◎   ◎

All the holy men seem to have gone off and died. There's no one left but us sinners to carry on the ministry.

Jamie Buckingham

◎   ◎   ◎

I take comfort from the fact that it was willing amateurs who built the ark, whereas professionals built the Titanic.

Seven Deadly Sins

E. Stanley Jones, an American missionary, statesman, author and lecturer, formulated what he called the seven deadly sins:

Politics without principle,
Wealth without work,
Pleasure without conscience,
Knowledge without character,
Business without morality,

Science without humanity,
Worship without sacrifice.

Shared Leadership

As a busy mother commented, "It took me a lot longer to make breakfast this morning. My children helped me!"

Sin

On the church notice board was a poster that read: "Are you tired of sin? Then come inside."

Underneath someone had added, "If not, phone Bayswater 23769."

◎　◎　◎

Sin: putting worst things first.

Joseph Gancher

◎　◎　◎

I'm more afraid of my own heart than of the Pope and all his cardinals!

Martin Luther

◎　◎　◎

You cannot play with sin and overcome it at the same time.

J. C. Macaulay

◎　◎　◎

Most of us spend the first six days of each week sowing wild oats and the seventh praying for a crop failure.

Sincerity

It was the great Methodist evangelist, John Wesley, who told his young preachers: "Don't worry about how to get crowds. Just get on fire and the people will come to see you burn."

Single-Mindedness

Don't grumble, don't bluster,
  don't dream and don't shirk,
Don't think of your worries,
  but think of your work.
The worries will vanish,
  the work will be done;
No man sees his shadow,
  who faces the sun.

Do all the good you can
By all the means you can
In all the ways you can
In all the places you can
At all the times you can
To all the people you can
As long as ever you can.

John Wesley

Sloth

Two men were walking along when one suddenly turned and stamped viciously on a snail.
  "What did you do that for?" asked the other.
  "Oh, it's been following me around all day!"

Society

In the United States in the 1990s, in any one day:

2795	teenage girls get pregnant
372	teenage girls miscarry
1106	teenage girls have an abortion
67	babies die before one month of life
105	children die from poverty
10	children are killed by guns
30	children are wounded by guns
135,000	children bring a gun to school
6	teenagers commit suicide
7742	teenagers become sexually active
623	teenagers get syphilis or gonorrhea
211	children are arrested for drug abuse
437	children are arrested for drinking or drunken driving
1512	children drop out of school
1849	children are abused or neglected
3288	children run away from home
1629	children are in adult jails
2556	children are born out of wedlock
2989	children see their parents divorced
34,285	people lose their jobs

We have stopped being a Christian country.

David Jenkins, Bishop of Durham, 1987

Sorrow

Lessons from Sorrow

I walked a mile with Pleasure;
She chatted all the way,
But left me none the wiser
For all she had to say.

I walked a mile with Sorrow
And ne'er a word said she;
But, oh, the things I learned from her
When Sorrow walked with me.

◎   ◎   ◎

Earth has no sorrow that heaven cannot heal.

Thomas Moore

◎   ◎   ◎

How else but through a broken heart
May Lord Christ enter in?

Oscar Wilde in "The Ballad of Reading Gaol"

Sovereignty of God

At a minister's induction, the order of service declared that the hymn before the Act of Induction would be "Our God re-signs."

◎   ◎   ◎

"Our Father who art in heaven, hallowed be thy name ..."

Spiritual Warfare

The *Encylopaedia Britannica* describes Joseph Lister, the nineteenth-century medic, as "the father of antiseptic surgery." During the course of his work, Lister was disturbed by the high proportion of patients who died after operations, not because of any problem with the operations themselves, but from post-operative infections.

He became convinced that infinitesimal microbes, invisible to the naked eye, were causing the infections. So he began to develop a number of antiseptic solutions with which to treat the wounds. Sure enough, the proportion of patients dying from infections decreased.

In the same way, there are evil spiritual forces at work in our world today. They cannot be seen, but they wreak havoc in people's lives, causing them to fall into temptation, moving evil men into positions of national power, manipulating people's emotions, tearing them apart and destroying them.

But just as Lister's contemporaries dismissed his theory of destructive microbes, many Christians today are ignorant or dismissive of spiritual realities. Yet we have the powerful spiritual "antiseptic" of prayer to use against them, and it is vital that we learn to do so.

Standing Up for the Faith

A police sergeant with a class of cadets asked, "Imagine you're on duty when two cars smash into each other. You are just about to go to their aid when you notice an articulated lorry heading down the hill toward this blind corner where the accident occurred. You hear a scream and see that the shock of the crash has sent a pregnant woman on the pavement into premature labor. Meanwhile, a fireball from one of the car's petrol tanks is heading towards a crowded pub full of underage drinkers. What do you do?"

An intelligent young cadet spoke up, "Slip off my uniform and merge with the crowd, sarge!"

A great oak is only a little nut that held its ground.

Stand-Ins

We're so glad you agreed to come today—we asked ten other preachers who said "no"!

◎ ◎ ◎

As the substitute preacher stood in the pulpit, he noticed a piece of old cardboard filling in the gap in a beautiful, but broken, stained-glass window.

"You know," he said, "standing in for such an eminent preacher today, I feel a bit like that cardboard in the stained-glass window—a poor substitute for the real thing."

After the service, one of the congregation greeted him warmly at the door: "I want you to know," he said, "that you weren't a piece of cardboard this morning—you were a real pane!"

◎ ◎ ◎

The curate had stepped in to take the sermon at very short notice, because the vicar was ill. At the end of the sermon he explained apologetically, "At such short notice I'm afraid I just had to rely on the Holy Spirit. Next week I hope to do better!"

Stewardship

The huge, brass offertory plates were passed around the congregation one Sunday evening—and returned almost empty to the vicar. He took them, held them up to heaven and prayed, "Lord, we thank you for the safe return of these plates . . ."

Stress

Leaders should always remember:
God loves you, and everyone else has a marvelous plan for your life!

◎ ◎ ◎

When the going gets tough,
the tough go shopping.

Success

If at first you don't succeed . . . so much for skydiving.

◎   ◎   ◎

Only in a dictionary does success come before work.

◎   ◎   ◎

Success is never final, failure never fatal. It's courage that counts.

◎   ◎   ◎

The worst that can happen to a man is to succeed before he is ready.

D. Martyn Lloyd-Jones

◎   ◎   ◎

When I try, I fail. When I trust, He succeeds.

Suffering

Job needed a doctor, but they sent him social workers!

◎   ◎   ◎

The Weaver

My life is but a weaving between my Lord and me,
I cannot choose the colors he worketh steadily.
Oft times he weaveth sorrow, and I in foolish pride
Forget he sees the upper and I the underside.

Not till the loom is silent and the shuttle ceased to fly,
Shall God unroll the canvas and explain the reason why
The dark threads are as needful in the weaver's skillful
hand,

As the threads of gold and silver, in the pattern he has
planned.

◎   ◎   ◎

When you struggle in the darkness, don't forget what you
heard in the light.

Sunday Trading

"The merchants and tradesmen camped outside Jerusalem
once or twice, but I spoke sharply to them and said, 'What
are you doing out here, camping round the wall? If you do
this again, I will arrest you.' And that was the last time they
came on the Sabbath."

Nehemiah 13:2–21, *The Living Bible*

Tact

Tact is the art of making a point without making an enemy.

Howard W. Newton

Teaching

One over the Edge

'Twas a dangerous cliff, as they freely confessed,
Though to walk near its crest was so pleasant;
But over its terrible edge there had slipped
A Duke and full many a peasant.
So the people said something would have to be done,
But their project did not at all tally;
Some said, "Put a fence round the edge of the cliff."
Some said, "An ambulance down in the valley."

And the cry for an ambulance carried the day,
For it spread to a neighboring city.
A fence may be useful or not, it is true,
But each heart became brim full of pity—

For those who slipped over the terrible cliff.
And the dwellers in highway and alley
Gave pounds or gave pence, not to put up a fence
But an ambulance down in the valley.

"For the cliff is all right, if you're careful," they said,
"And if folks ever slip and are dropping,
It isn't the slipping that hurts them so much
As the shock down below when they're stopping!"

So day after day, as the mishaps occurred,
Quick forth would rescuers sally,
To pick up the victims who fell from the cliff,
With an ambulance down in the valley.

Better guard well the young than reclaim them when old,
For the voice of true wisdom is calling;
To rescue the fallen is good, but 'tis best
To prevent other people from falling.

Better close up the source of temptation and crime
Than deliver from dungeon and galley;
Better build a strong fence round the top of the cliff,
Than an ambulance down in the valley!

Teamwork

Fred's never been much of a sportsman. When he played
goalie in football, the team called him Cinderella because
he kept missing the ball.

Temptation

It is startling to think that Satan can actually come into the heart of a man in such close touch with Jesus as Judas was. And more—he is cunningly trying to do it today. Yet he can only get in through a door opened from the inside. Every man controls the door of his own life. Satan can't get in without our help.

S. D. Gordon

◎   ◎   ◎

When you flee temptation, be sure you don't leave a forwarding address!

Thinking

As long as the devil can keep us terrified of thinking, he will always limit the work of God in our souls.

Oswald Chambers

◎   ◎   ◎

If God had meant Christians to think, he'd have given them brains.

◎   ◎   ◎

Reading molds thinking. As I scan my shelves I spot those books other than the Bible that have influenced my personal thought and ministry, particularly my battle not to become secularized. Unless we maintain constant companionship with Christians who direct our thinking Christianly, we easily fall prey to the spirit of the times.

Katie Funk Wiebe

◎   ◎   ◎

A great many people think they are thinking wh(
merely rearranging their prejudices.

Willi;

Thoroughness

He went through it like a twelve-year-old inspecting his mustache.

Tradition

Tradition is the living faith of the dead. Honor it! Traditionalism is the dead faith of the living. Abandon it!

Transformation

The audience was waiting for the brilliant pianist to come out onto the stage. Then, to everyone's embarrassment, a little boy wandered up onto the stage and started banging out one harsh note on the *Steinway*. Suddenly, the maestro appeared in the wings and made his way over to the boy.

Standing behind him as he banged away tunelessly, he began to weave a melody around the note, taking it up into his larger tune and transforming it into something beautiful. After a few moments, the maestro gently led the boy away from the piano, and together they took a bow to the audience's applause. The little boy wandered back to his seat—not embarrassed, not having been made to look foolish.

In the same way, Jesus can take the harsh, discordant, out-of-tune moments of our lives—perhaps a time of sexual sin, or of cowardice or defeat in some other way—and can weave his own purposes around them. As we let him do this, he transforms our mistakes and failures, bringing out of them something he can use for his glory.

Translations

A Russian interpreter, not knowing what to make of "The spirit is willing but the flesh is weak," translated it, "The vodka is good but the meat is bad!"

Trust

Never trust a man who, when left alone in a room with a tea cosy, doesn't try it on.

A man fell off a cliff but managed to grab hold of a branch on his way down. He hung there and shouted up to the top, "Is anybody up there?"
  "Yes," came the reply, "God is up here!"
  "Can you help me, God?"
  "Yes."
  "What do you want me to do?"
  "Let go of the branch."
  There was a pause.
  "Is there anybody else up there?"

Even if you think you have someone eating out of your hand, it's still advisable to count your fingers afterwards!

There's only one thing better than a friend you can trust, and that's a friend who trusts you.

Truth

A lie can travel halfway around the world while the truth is putting on its shoes.

Mark Twain

Men occasionally stumble over the truth, but most of them pick themselves up and hurry off as if nothing had happened.

Sir Winston Churchill

Values—Relative and Absolute

Norman was the man at the factory who sounded the horn to say when work began and finished. Every morning as he walked past the jewellers, he set his watch by the big clock in the window. One day his watch went wrong, so on the way home from work, he took it into the jewellers for mending. Next morning he picked it up, and as he was leaving the shop, he set his watch by the big clock in the window.

"Yes, I know that's always right," said the watchmaker. "I set it every morning by the factory horn."

Verbosity

In a small trumpet blast against bureaucratic verbosity, this list is circulating around government departments in Washington:

The Lord's Prayer: 56 words.

The twenty-third Psalm: 118 words.

The Gettysburg Address: 226 words.

The Ten Commandments: 297 words.

The USDA order on the price of cabbage: 15,629 words.

Vision

We think too small, like the frog at the bottom of the well. He thinks the sky is only as big as the top of the well. If he surfaced, he would have an entirely different view.

Mao Tse-tung

◎　◎　◎

Our task now is not to fix the blame for the past, but to fix the course for the future.

John F. Kennedy

◎　◎　◎

The man who misses all the fun
Is he who says, "It can't be done."
In solemn pride, he stands aloof
And greets each venture with reproof.
Had he the power, he would efface
The history of the human race.
We'd have no radio, no cars,
No streets lit by electric stars;
No telegraph, no telephone;
We'd linger in the age of stone.
The world would sleep if things were run
By folks who say, "It can't be done."

◎　◎　◎

It is for us to pray, not for tasks equal to our powers, but for powers equal to our tasks; to go forward with a great desire forever beating at the door of our hearts as we travel toward our distant goal.

Helen Keller

War

I confess without shame that I am tired and sick of the war. Its glory is all moonshine. Even victory the most brilliant is over dead and mangled bodies, the anguish and lamentation of distant families crying out to me for missing sons, husbands and fathers. It is only those who have not heard the shrieks and groans of the wounded and lacerated, that clamor for more blood, more vengeance, more desolation.

William Tecumseh Sherman, Civil War general

Will

The secret of an unsettled life lies too often in an unsurrendered will.

Will of God

When David Livingstone was asked if he was afraid that going into Africa would be too difficult and too dangerous, he answered, "I am immortal until the will of God for me is accomplished."

Wisdom

There had never been any argument about it: Fred was the wisest and shrewdest man in town. One day a young lad in the community questioned him about it.

"Fred, what is it that makes you so wise?" he asked.

"Good judgment," replied Fred, readily. "I'd say it was my good judgment."

"And where did you get your good judgment?"

"That I got from experience."

"Where did you get your experience?"

"From my bad judgment."

A pilot came aboard a large tanker to help bring it into harbor. The captain asked him if he really knew where all the rocks were. "No," he replied, "but I know where there aren't any!"

Witness

The sixteenth-century bishop Hugh Latimer was one of the first preachers of social righteousness in the English-speaking world. He was imprisoned for his denunciations of social and ecclesiastical abuses. While in the Tower of London he wrote, "Pray for me; I say, pray for me. At times I am so afraid that I could creep into a mousehole." This was the same Latimer who later walked bravely to the stake in Oxford, saying to his companion, Nicholas Ridley, as he went, "Play the man, Master Ridley; we shall this day light such a candle, by God's grace, in England, as I trust shall never be put out."

Women

The Baptist church deacons decided to invite their woman minister to go fishing with them. They were fifty yards or so from the shore when she said apologetically, "I'm sorry—I've forgotten my fishing rod!"

So she hopped out of the boat, walked across the water to the bank and picked up the rod. As she strolled back one deacon muttered, "Typical of a woman—always forgetting things!"

Wonder

The most beautiful and the most profound emotion we can experience is the sensation of the mystical. It is the power of all true science. He to whom this emotion is a stranger, who can no longer wonder and stand rapt in awe, is as good as dead.

Albert Einstein

Words

I try to watch the words I say,
And keep them soft and sweet;
For I don't know from day to day,
Which ones I'll have to eat!

Work

The pope was asked on one occasion, "How many people work here at the Vatican?" He replied, "Oh, about half of them."

Worldliness

The Christian is not ruined by living in the world but by the world living in him.

Worry

Ulcers are caused not by what you eat, but by what's eating you!

◎   ◎   ◎

You can't change the past, but you can spoil the present by worrying about the future.

◎   ◎   ◎

When I look back on all these worries, I remember the story of the old man who said, on his deathbed, that he had a lot of trouble in his life, most of which never happened.

Sir Winston Churchill

Worship

The Danish philosopher Kierkegaard compared worship to a dramatic production.

In worship, it often seems as though the worship leader is the actor and God is the prompter, whispering into his ear, telling him what to do next. The congregation listen and, at the end, they applaud if they like the way he's led worship or throw things if they don't!

But, Kierkegaard said, that's all backward. In reality, God is the audience, the congregation the actors, and the person leading worship is the prompter, simply keeping the production going.

So when we come together to worship, we come wanting to please God alone, offering to him our very best.

◎　　◎　　◎

Seen on a church noticeboard: "You aren't too bad to come in; you aren't too good to stay out!"

Young People

Some things never change . . .
The children now love luxury; they show disrespect for elders and love chatter in the place of exercise. Children are tyrants, not the servants of their households. They no longer rise when their elders enter the room. They contradict their parents, chatter before company, gobble up dainties at the table, cross their legs and tyrannize their teachers.

Socrates, 469–399 BC

I see no hope for the future of our people if they are dependent on the frivolous youth of today, for certainly all youth are reckless beyond words . . . When I was young, we were taught to be discreet and respectful of elders, but the present youth are exceedingly impatient of restraint.

Hesiod, Greek poet, eighth-century BC

Stephen Gaukroger is the senior minister of Stopsley Baptist Church, Luton, England, and author of many books, including *It Makes Sense, Making It Work, Growing Your Gifts, Hunger for Holiness,* and *Thirsty for God.*

Nick Mercer is assistant principal of London Bible College, where he is also director of training.